Al Stewart has given us a robu
explanation of the challenges
and confusing world. For many of us, this is exactly what ....

Gary Millar
Principal, Queensland Theological College

This is a great book! It's full of thoughtful insights that challenge cultural assumptions and give a much better story of what it is to be a man. Inspirational. God's vision for men is powerfully good. A must-read.

Andrew Heard
Lead Pastor, EV Church, Erina

Gender confusion and identity lostness is littering our social landscape with an unspeakable toll. Al Stewart's *Manual* is jam-packed with biblical fidelity, cultural astuteness and pastoral sensitivity. It's courageous yet tender. Theologically deep yet accessible. A desperately needed book to rescue men, families, churches and societies for the wholesomeness of life that Jesus beautifully redeems us for. A must for every family and church.

Christopher Chia
Senior Pastor, Adam Road Presbyterian Church, Singapore

I'm trying to raise three boys to be men who follow Jesus and give up their lives for the sake of those around them, as well as working with men—young and old—across the country who are striving to do the same. In a sea of confusion as to what it looks like to be a man today, this is the book I'm going to give them from now on. Clear, biblical and desperately needed.

Derek Hanna
General Manager, Geneva Push church-planting network

Al Stewart has done us a great service by courageously exploring the minefield of 21st-century masculinity. He engages with popular culture, expert opinion and the Bible, while helpfully bringing to bear decades of accumulated wisdom. I found his definition of healthy masculinity to be an insightful touchstone for my own life and relationships. Over the last

20 years, I have stopped reading books like this because I generally come away discouraged. Not this time. I was still challenged, but I was encouraged, too. I could also immediately think of plenty of people I wanted to give the book to, including my sons, daughter, daughters-in-law, and the men's breakfast group I belong to.

Paul Harrington
Senior Pastor, Trinity Network, Adelaide

Al Stewart has boldly gone where angels fear to tread. He has sought to expose toxic masculinity in all its ugliness and replace it with a biblically grounded, Christ-shaped framework. This book is a call for boys (young or old) to be men of God who understand they are empowered to love, serve, and protect others within the context of their God-given relationships. You may not agree with every point Al makes, but you will be seriously challenged and inspired to reconsider a healthy vision of masculinity.

Ray Galea
Lead Pastor, Fellowship Church of Dubai

Christian books on masculinity tend to fall into one of two camps. Some are thinly guised Christianized versions of masculinity taken from popular culture and Western stereotypes. And others are so keen to label all masculinity 'toxic' that they leave men feeling inherently worthless. Al's book is neither. In *The Manual,* he builds a compelling case for masculine identity, grounded in Scripture and supported by social, scientific and psychological research. Al is ready to call out the sins of men, the distorting effects of culture, and toxic masculinity. But he does so without throwing the whole project of being a man under the bus in the process. Instead, he gives us a powerful and practical vision of what restored and redeemed masculinity could look like. A great book for men's groups, Bible studies, and fathers to read with their sons. Highly recommended.

Rory Shiner
Senior Pastor, Providence Church, Perth

I'm a reluctant reader of men's self-help books. To be honest, Al Stewart is the person who's given me a number of them to read over the years, pushing me to reflect on my work, loving my wife, leading my family and being a better boss. I'd much rather listen to a Jack Reacher novel or get lost in a non-fiction history book. But I found myself quickly moving to the next chapter of *The Manual*. Al has this ability to simply reflect on our current culture and with great care encourage me to man up and make a difference with the people I care about most. Importantly (and as always), he's pushed me to reflect on God's word anew. Like Al, this book is practical. Read it with others. Reflect on it. Put it into practice.

Scott Sanders
Executive Director, Reach Australia

As a woman, I think Al Stewart does indeed "get masculinity right". Power used to serve is a theme that runs throughout the book. In an age where men face so many conflicting messages, *The Manual* helpfully paints a picture of what it looks like to be an adult man rather than an adult boy. What a blessing this type of man is to all those around him!

This insightful, enjoyable and easy-to-read book is helpful for young and old, Christians and those who don't yet believe. It highlights how truly following the greatest man shows men their value and gives them purpose in life.

Sue Harrington
Board member, Reach Australia

I have loved reading this book. It is firmly biblically grounded. It is packed with practical and carefully applied wisdom. It is full of thorough and well-documented research. At no stage does the author leave the reader crippled by guilt. Grace and gospel incentive drive everything. To cap it all, it is entertaining and fun to read. I will encourage many men and women at St Helen's to read it.

William Taylor
St Helen's Bishopsgate, London

AL STEWART

THE MANUAL

GETTING
MASCULINITY
RIGHT

matthiasmedia
SYDNEY · YOUNGSTOWN

The Manual
© Al Stewart 2022

Matthias Media
(St Matthias Press Ltd ACN 067 558 365)
Email: info@matthiasmedia.com.au
Internet: www.matthiasmedia.com.au
Please visit our website for current postal and telephone contact information.

Matthias Media (USA)
Email: sales@matthiasmedia.com
Internet: www.matthiasmedia.com
Please visit our website for current postal and telephone contact information.

ISBN 978 1 925424 71 3

Cover design and typesetting by Lankshear Design.

FOREWORD

O UR BOYS ARE IN trouble, and they are growing into men who are in trouble.

And when one sex is in trouble, neither sex is doing as well as it could. Western countries are more anxious, divided, distrustful and tribalized than ever, and a big part of the problem—lost and confused men—is largely ignored by those who have the megaphones and the cultural heft in these times.

The raw statistics tell the story. In the United States, for example, men between 25 and 31 are a staggering 66 percent more likely than women to be living with their parents.[1] The US prison population—which increased by more than 700 percent between 1973 and 2013—is 93 percent male and disproportionately young.[2] Every day, 150 workers die from hazardous working conditions, and 92 percent of them are male.[3] By the eighth grade, 41 percent of girls are at least proficient in writing, while only 20 percent of boys are.[4] Elsewhere, a large study from Britain finds that boys' IQs have dropped by about 15 percent since the 1980s.[5]

In their important book *The Boy Crisis*, Warren Farrell and John Gray present us with a confronting diagnosis. They write:

1 W Farrell and J Gray, *The Boy Crisis: Why our boys are struggling and what we can do about it*, BenBella Books, 2018, p 2.
2 Farrell and Gray, *The Boy Crisis*, p 17.
3 Farrell and Gray, *The Boy Crisis*, p 21.
4 Farrell and Gray, *The Boy Crisis*, p 28.
5 Farrell and Gray, *The Boy Crisis*, p 421, n11.

"the most important single crisis in developed countries [is] dad-deprived children, and especially dad-deprived boys".[6] An astonishing 85 percent of US youths in prison grew up in father-less homes;[7] 90 percent of US male prisoners are father-deprived, as are 85 percent of mass shooters.

As Farrell and Gray point out, researchers have shown that mothers are good at setting boundaries, but fathers are better at enforcing them. In other words, huge numbers of children are brought up without firm boundaries. They particularly lack the ability to delay gratification—and so make bad short-term choices which limit longer-term flourishing.

Both boys and girls suffer across some fifty areas of life in the absence of a father—health, education, discipline and self-esteem being a few—but boys suffer more severely. And as Farrell and Gray document, when boys are hurt, they hurt us—physically, psychologically and economically.

Even when boys do manage a decent level of educational attainment, they are often less likely to obtain a job and likely to earn less than their female counterparts. In 147 of America's biggest cities, women in their twenties are not only more likely than men of the same age to find a job as the emerging employment market favours women; they are also earning more than men of the same age.[8]

In Australian society, young men are under-represented in Australian university enrolments, with females accounting for 58 percent of all students in 2016.[9] The proportion of female postgraduates is even higher. Sadly, men are significantly over-

6   Farrell and Gray, *The Boy Crisis*, p 102.
7   Farrell and Gray, *The Boy Crisis*, p 120.
8   Farrell and Gray, *The Boy Crisis*, p 120.
9   FP Larkins, *Male students remain underrepresented in Australian universities. Should we be concerned?*, University of Melbourne website, 2018, accessed 25 October 2021 (melbourne-cshe.unimelb.edu.au/lh-martin-institute/insights/gender-enrolment-trends-flarkins).

represented in the suicide rate. In 2017, 2,348 Australian men took their own lives.[10] This figure was up a massive 10 percent on 2016 and is *three times* the female suicide rate.[11] Men are also dramatically over-represented in the Australian prison population: Corrective Services Australia reported in 2021 that 92 percent of the prison population was male (39,768 inmates).[12]

It is a good thing that so many young women are doing well, of course, but it is producing even more confusion in the minds of young men. What place is there for the protector–provider instincts that are so deeply embedded in men? And how are they to respond when they come to feel that their masculinity is not only seen by many as toxic, but something that is in and of itself toxic? Many spiral downwards into depression, anxiety and addiction of various kinds—all too often on the road to prison or, worse, self-harm.

Al Stewart understands very well what is happening. He cares deeply about every wasted and damaged life, and he sees the factors creating the mess. He has written an extremely accessible and very readable 'manual' for men trying to break free from their failings and inadequacies and become the best they can.

Importantly, he in no way excuses bad behaviour. Indeed, he condemns it—but in offering solutions he does a very effective and much-needed demolition job on bad solutions. It is madness to try and imply, as so many do today, that masculinity is by definition toxic. Rather, as Al confirms, true masculinity is as wonderful and important as true femininity.

As he puts it: "Masculinity is fundamentally about *how* men

10 G Poole, Male *suicides in Australia up 10 per cent in 2017,* Australian Men's Health Forum website, 2019, accessed 25 October 2021 (amhf.org.au/male_suicides_in_australia_up_10_in_2017).
11 Poole, *Male suicides in Australia up 10 per cent in 2017.*
12 Australian Bureau of Statistics, *Corrective Services, Australia,* ABS website, June 2021, accessed 25 October 2021 (abs.gov.au/statistics/people/crime-and-justice/corrective-services-australia/jun-quarter-2021).

use their power. When it is done in a healthy way, masculinity will serve and bless those it touches." He quotes Steve Biddulph, who observes that "boys care about themselves" while "men care about others". And he makes the telling observation that he has met 50-year-old boys and 18-year-old men.

We must break the cycle of lostness and brokenness in our boys and our men, and better fathering and father-figuring is a vital key to this imperative. Al Stewart makes a most exceptional father figure, as I see it, and this book is a must-read, a must-ponder-over, for it is truly insightful, wise and practical.

The Hon John Anderson AO FTSE
Former Deputy Prime Minister of Australia

CONTENTS

To the men of Bridge Street Fellowship:

Thanks for your patience as I've spoken about these topics over the years, and for your wisdom as we've sharpened one another.

"Iron sharpens iron,
and one man sharpens another."
(Proverbs 27:17, HSBC)

INTRODUCTION

I T MAY SEEM STRANGE to begin a book with an apology, but I wish I could apologize in person to the young man who asked me a question at a men's convention in 2017. I was one of the speakers in a question-and-answer session, and in a room of more than 100 blokes he asked, "What does it mean to be a man? Today it seems so confusing, and I don't know what I'm supposed to do."

At the time I didn't take his question seriously, and instead I answered him in clichés about 'masculine' activities and attitudes. I'm sorry. I hope he picks up this book, because it's an attempt to answer his question and the question of so many young men I speak to: How do I live a life of healthy masculinity?

As I try to do this, I want to be up front with you. It's inevitable that in the following pages my crusty-old-bloke perspectives are going to shine through. I have been known to have a rant every now and then. But please remember: the fact that they're old and crusty doesn't mean they're necessarily wrong. Our own views on gender—and, in this case, masculinity—are so shaped by our background and experiences that it's impossible to be completely objective about these matters. This is as true for you as it is for me. We all have our own blind spots and assumptions. So I'll try to be honest about what my personal opinions are, and trust you'll be discerning enough to weigh up what I have to say.

Wading into the gender wars between progressives and conservatives, between feminists and men's rights groups, is about as inviting as sticking your head into a bag full of angry cats. But my goal isn't to fight that battle, or to resolve the gender, transgender, and no-gender problems. My goal is more concrete than that and, I think, more achievable. I want to talk to you, the man reading this book, about what it means to live a life that is spiritually healthy, filled with strength and power and purpose. I want to talk about what it means to 'man up'.

Does that sound a bit dodgy to you? A bit toxic, perhaps? Well, let me tell you what I mean by that.

'Power' is a tricky word today, and we're rightly suspicious of people who crave it. But what I mean by 'power' is *the ability or opportunity to care for those around you.* I want you to be aware of the power you have to make a positive difference in the world. You might affect only a small part of the world, but you will make a real difference in the part of the world that matters most to you—the place where you live with the people you care about. To man up there will make a huge difference to those closest to you, because whatever strength you possess will be directed towards caring for them.

Here's what the *Oxford Advanced Learner's Dictionary* tells us it means to 'man up':

> **man up** (informal):
> *to start being brave or strong in order to deal with a difficult situation*

But this definition only supplies part of the picture. To genuinely man up in the way that I'm talking about will cost you. To put it another way, a life of healthy masculinity will always have a self-sacrificial element to it. It might feel like a crunch in gears at first, but healthy masculinity and love go together because real love means putting other people before yourself. Real love involves caring for the people around you, and that takes effort. It will cost you time, money, sleep and a thousand other things. It will require discipline, self-control and self-denial. Yet it will be a life in which you know who you are, and what matters to you. You'll live like a man who's worked out what matters and *who* matters, and you'll put that knowledge into practice in well-thought-out ways every day. That's the sort of power I'd like to see operating in your life.

More than that, though, I want you to have a life of purpose. It's no good having the grit and determination to powerfully love those around you if you lack a compass to guide your efforts. And when I talk about a life of purpose, I want to look at what it means to live in the way that God our Creator wants us to live. If you're not a follower of Jesus, wouldn't it make sense to look at what the most influential man who ever lived wants men to be like? If you are already one of his followers, you'll know that he's definitely worth listening to—in fact, he's worth giving your life to. But if you're not there yet—if you're still kicking tyres and rubbing your chin about Jesus and this idea of faith—that's okay too. I hope this book helps you not only to become a powerful, purpose-filled man, but also to see what the Bible says about being Jesus' man, and why that's the best way to live.

———

So how does *The Manual* work?

In the first six chapters, I look at masculinity in our world—at the confusion in our society around what masculinity really is, at the devaluing of masculinity, and then at what our Creator says about healthy masculinity. I've included two chapters on how to look after 'future you' and on the power of the ordinary, day-by-day life.

In the next six chapters, I look at the specifics of living as a man. My focus switches to the different roles that men have (such as son, friend or husband) and how we express healthy masculinity in those roles as we invest in the lives of others. Even if not all of these chapters apply to you right now, I'd still urge you to read them all (though it's fine to jump around a bit and start with the ones that are most relevant to you). For one thing, it will help you understand what life is like for other men around you. More importantly, all these chapters work together to give an overall picture of healthy masculinity. This book has a long-term aim: to help shape us into the kind of men who understand God's idea of manhood as presented in the Bible, and to help us grab hold of God's wisdom for living as men. Each of these chapters will, I hope, give you a piece of that puzzle.

At the end of the book, I look at what it means to follow the greatest man, Jesus Christ, and so find life now and in eternity.

PART ONE

THE SEARCH FOR HEALTHY MASCULINITY

1. MASCULINITY: CONFUSION REIGNS

A FEW YEARS AGO, I arranged a once-in-a-lifetime hunting trip to Cape York (the pointy end of Queensland) with my Dad and my brother. We were going to spend a week hunting feral pigs on a cattle station that's spread across almost 3,000 square kilometres—think of something the size of greater Sydney but with just a handful of people living there. We had to fly to the property on the weekly mail plane from Cairns, which is about 600 km away. When we landed on the property's airstrip around mid-morning we were met by Bob, who was about the same age as my Dad and who ran the hunting and safari business for soft city boys like us. As our gear and the station's weekly groceries were being unloaded from the plane, the property owner, Dave, pulled up on a motorbike. Just behind him, another bloke pulled up in a beat-up, open-top four-wheel drive. Dave, with his mane of shaggy hair and black bushy beard, was approximately the same size and shape as a grizzly bear. He was also barefoot. He looked the three of us up and down and said with a lazy smile, "G'day". When he saw I was looking at his choice of footwear, he said, "Yeah, I spilled acid on my boots a few weeks ago and I haven't gone into town yet to pick up another pair".[1]

Dave explained that he and the driver of the four-wheel drive

1   I've changed the names of Bob and Dave to protect their privacy and also my life.

(who was even bigger than Dave) had been out that day catching scrub bulls. Scrub bulls are feral cattle that have been wild for generations. The way Dave and his mate caught them, I'm told, is pretty standard. You take a four-wheel drive, or a quad bike if a four-wheel drive isn't available, and strap old tyres to the bull bar. You chase the bull through the bush at high speed until it's exhausted, then knock it over. While the bull is trying to get up, you jump out and tie its back legs together. Then you tie it by the horns to a tree and untie its back legs. Simple, right? Later on, you come back with a truck to pick up all the bulls you've caught, dragging them into the truck with a winch. Then it's off to the cattle yard. Once the yard is full, a semitrailer comes out and loads them up for the long trip to the sale yards. Catching scrub bulls is not for the fainthearted.

So that was our welcome to Cape York.

One night, about halfway through our trip, we were having dinner in the huge corrugated iron shed where we slept each night. There were six of us around the trestle table: Bob, Dave, Dave's giant mate (whose day job was flying around in a helicopter shooting feral animals in the nearby national park), my brother, my Dad, and me. We had just eaten a bucketload of spaghetti bolognese (and I do mean a bucket—they'd used a 20-litre tub to cook it all). There was a forest of empty beer bottles on the table, and six sauce-smeared plates. With a full belly and a beer in hand, Dave looked at us three visitors and asked, "So, what do you blokes do for a living?" After a pause, my father leaned forward and slowly answered, "Well, I'm a retired prison officer. Mark is a carpenter. And Alan is ..." Dad looked up and our eyes met above the beer bottles. The look on his face told me he didn't know what else to say. He shrugged and looked apologetic. "Alan is an Anglican minister."

I had not been aware of the crickets chirping outside until that moment. As we sat in silence, I wondered what it was I'd really wanted my father to say. Maybe "Alan is an officer in the SAS", or "Alan works on an oil rig", or "Alan is a champion rodeo rider". There was so much testosterone in the air that night that it felt like I needed a job masculine enough for me to keep my man-card.

But is that really what masculinity is? Is it being tough? Strong? Is it being able to wrestle wild cattle? Does it only come in one shape? How do you actually get your man-card, and how do you keep it? What does it really look like to man up?

The great confusion

Leonard Sax is a medical doctor and psychologist with a bachelor's degree in biology, a PhD in psychology, and years of experience in patient care. He is deeply concerned about what's happening in our society at the moment in the area of gender:

> One hundred years from now, scholars may look back at the cultural disintegration manifest in the first half of the twenty-first century and conclude that a fundamental cause of the unravelling of our social fabric was the neglect of gender in the raising of our children. I wonder what those future historians will say about how long it took us to recognize our mistake, to realize that what girls need is different from what boys need—to understand that gender matters.[2]

Whether or not historians will be pondering our cultural disintegration in a hundred years, I can't say. I do suspect, though, that the average person will wonder whether there was something in the water that was making us crazy. Few topics have generated such heat or confusion as the 21st-century debates over sex,

2   L Sax, *Why Gender Matters: What parents and teachers need to know about the emerging science of sex differences,* 2nd edn, Harmony Books, 2017, p 314.

gender and male–female relations. There are too many examples to list here, but let's highlight a few to make the point.

In December 2018, tennis legend and LGBTI ambassador Martina Navratilova "stumbled into a hornets' nest"[3] (to use her own words) when she made the following statement about biological males participating in women's sport: "Clearly that can't be right. You can't just proclaim yourself a female and be able to compete against women. There must be some standards, and having a penis and competing as a woman would not fit that standard."[4] Navratilova was smashed on social media for making this 'outrageous' claim, and subsequently apologized for any offence given.

In 2019, a Canadian court ruled against Jonathan 'Jessica' Yaniv, a transgender woman who made international news by bringing discrimination complaints against 15 female beauty technicians who refused to wax his male genitals. The court ruled that the beauty technicians had the right to refuse to deal with male genitalia, because "human rights legislation does not require a service provider to wax a type of genitals they are not trained for and have not consented to wax".[5]

The gender debate has become so fraught that the play *The Vagina Monologues* has been banned at some women's colleges in the USA, because it is now argued that "a play about women who have vaginas excludes transwomen, who don't have vaginas".[6]

It's not just about the potential offence that can now be caused by defining genders. The very concepts of male and female are

3   Starts at 60 Writers, 'Martina Navratilova apologises for transgender "cheat" comments', *Starts at 60*, 4 March 2019, accessed 7 January 2022 (startsat60.com/discover/news/martina-navratilova-apologises-for-transgender-women-in-sport-comments).

4   J Vigo, 'Confronting a new threat to female athletics', *Quillette*, 27 February 2019, accessed 7 January 2022 (quillette.com/2019/02/27/confronting-a-new-threat-to-female-athletics).

5   *Yaniv v Various Waxing Salons (No. 2)* [2019] BCHRT 222 [British Columbia Human Rights Tribunal decision] at 15, accessed 7 January 2022 (bchrt.bc.ca/law-library/decisions/2019/oct.htm).

6   Sax, *Why Gender Matters*, p 289.

under attack by academics, as we can see in the following example:

> Judith Butler is a professor at the University of California at
> Berkeley. She believes that we should challenge the "tradi-
> tional" division of the human race into male and female. In
> the name of personal freedom, Professor Butler encourages
> individuals to construct their own gender identity, without
> regard to their biological sex. According to Butler, notions
> such as "boy" and "girl," "man" and "woman," "father" and
> "mother" are all mere inventions of a sexist society created
> in order to support the patriarchy and 'heteronormativity'—
> the preference for straight people over gay and lesbian
> people (Butler herself is a lesbian).[7]

So while some are debating the differences between the genders,
others seem to be questioning their very existence. In fact, there
seems to be a concerted push to dissolve the concept of gender
difference altogether, especially where appearance is concerned.
For example, it seems that more and more men now dress
in traditionally feminine ways. American internet personality
James Charles has over 24 million subscribers to his YouTube
channel, which shows James applying make-up to himself with a
distinctly feminine result.[8] Or there's Clementine Ford, a feminist
author based in Melbourne, who says she wants to raise her son
to choose sparkly shoes and wear a dress if he chooses: "To the
boys who want butterflies painted on their cheeks, the boys who
twirl in dresses and the boys who always pick the sparkly shoes:
we can do this together. Are you ready? Love, Mummy."[9]

Is it any wonder so many young blokes are confused?

---

7   Sax, *Why Gender Matters*, pp 282-283.
8   See, for example, J Charles, 'Holiday slay makeup tutorial' [video], *James Charles*, YouTube, 22 November 2017, accessed 7 January 2022 (youtube.com/watch?v=BQC09Mdn24w).
9   C Ford, *Boys Will Be Boys: Power, patriarchy and the toxic bonds of mateship*, Allen & Unwin, 2018, p 364.

The results of our confusion

Leonard Sax has lived in the eye of this storm for decades. He has seen, diagnosed and helped thousands of boys and girls of all ages (as well as their families) to grapple with the gender issue. His experience and study has led him to the view that:

> We do no one any favors by pretending that these male/female differences do not exist. Ignoring reality always comes at a cost …
>
> Gender is more fragile than we knew. Though perhaps we should have known better. Most cultures have taken great care in teaching gender norms. We no longer do. On the contrary, our learned professors now actively deconstruct and tear down every gender guidepost, in the name of individual liberty, with no awareness of the costs. We need to be careful about the norms we teach, of course. We don't want to perpetuate stereotypes like the dumb jock or the dumb blonde. We need to create new ideals of manhood and womanhood that make sense in the twenty-first century. But "personhood" won't fly. Boys don't want to be "persons." Neither do girls. Boys want to be men. Girls want to be women. We have to teach them what that means.[10]

By "personhood", I take it that Dr Sax means human identity without reference to gender, or with the concept of gender removed. His conclusion is that gender is a key part of our identity as humans, and pretending it isn't, in his own words, "won't fly".

As if to underline Dr Sax's thesis, there is a growing problem in many countries relating to disengaged young men. In Japan, there are a large number of boys who are mockingly known as 'herbivores' (*soshokukei danshi*):

---

10 Sax, *Why Gender Matters*, pp 282, 288.

Herbivores spend almost as much on cosmetics and clothes as women. One company alone (WishRoom) has sold more than five thousand *bras* to these boys. Herbivores, also called "parasite singles" (*parasaito shinguru*), are typically apathetic about careers, dating, sex, and marriage. The herbivore typically lives with his parents. He is especially close to his mom.

This trend of maternal closeness and dependency is increasingly common throughout Western Europe. In Germany boys may be derided as nest-sitters (*Nesthocker*) for living at "Hotel Mama"; in Italy boys increasingly return home at their mother's encouragement, even as they (and sisters who accompany them) may be mocked as *bamboccioni* (big babies). In Greece and Spain, the youth unemployment rate exceeds 50 percent (versus 12 percent for US youth), replacing millions of young men's traditional sense of purpose with a sense of dependency.[11]

Some of us may be wondering if these boys mentioned above are a little short on testosterone. Testosterone is a controversial subject these days, and a full discussion of its effects on the male body and male behaviour is beyond the scope of this book. Instead, I'll offer a brief summary of Carole Hooven's scientifically thorough book, *Testosterone*. Hooven explains the science behind what many people might regard as common knowledge or even common sense—namely, the huge effect that testosterone has on the bodies and lives of boys and men.

Hooven summarizes as follows:

11 Farrell and Gray, *The Boy Crisis*, pp 56-57 (emphasis original). See also H Mirafiori, 'Japan: Herbivore men who sit when the [*sic*] pee emerge as economy worsens', *Economy Watch*, 18 June 2009, accessed 7 January 2022 (economywatch.com/2009/06/18/japan-herbivore-men-who-sit-when-the-pee-emerge-as-economy-worsens).

The effects of T [testosterone] are deep and wide-ranging. Boys' preference for rough-and-tumble play and men's motivation to compete with other men, their greater libido and preference for sexual novelty, and their athletic advantage over women are all testosterone derived. ... T levels in healthy men and women do not come close to overlapping: men's are 10-20 times those of women. In puberty, the gap in testosterone level is even wider—pubertal boys have about thirty times as much testosterone as girls.[12]

The effects of those higher levels of testosterone span the extremes—from terrible violence to heroic sacrifice:

Although the ratios for each country vary, men commit about 90 percent of physical assaults [injuring another person on purpose] but only about 80 percent of thefts [when the theft involves more physical risk, like stealing a car or breaking into a home, the number is higher].[13]

So men are more likely to commit violent crime. But men are also more likely to risk their lives in trying to save others, even strangers. Hooven gives the example of the Carnegie Hero Medal:

Since 1904, in the United States and Canada about ten thousand people have been awarded the Carnegie Hero Medal, which goes to a civilian who voluntarily risks his or her own life knowingly, to an extraordinary degree while saving or attempting to save the life of another person. ... About ten percent have gone to women. Recipients have saved people from drowning, from house fires, from animal attacks, and so on.[14]

12 C Hooven, *Testosterone: The story of the hormone that dominates and divides us*, Cassell, 2021, p 246.
13 Hooven, *Testosterone*, p 165.
14 Hooven, *Testosterone*, p 242.

Hooven analyses at some length writers (especially journalists) who wish to deny testosterone's effects on the male brain and male physiology. She says that this reluctance to accept the natural and physical explanation is because of the "naturalistic fallacy". Hooven quotes scientist and author Steven Pinker, who explains that this fallacy is based on a false view of 'nature'—"the belief that 'whatever happens in nature is good'". But Hooven continues: "It's not called a 'fallacy' for nothing. 'Natural diseases' like malaria are not in any way good. Nature is full of wonderful things, but it's also full of truly awful things."[15]

Hooven also explains that even though testosterone may tend to make men more violent or aggressive, they are still very much responsible for their actions. She speaks about her own son's journey into puberty and finishes the book with this insight:

> Because of the testosterone that he is on the way to producing, Griffin will likely differ from most women in many of the ways I've described in this book. Becoming a man is a beautiful thing. But—like every man—my son should enjoy his testosterone responsibly.[16]

So men are capable of great good and great evil, and every man must make his own decisions about how he will act. I still remember sitting with the front page of *The Australian* newspaper in front of me in early 2019 and reading about the award given to Drs Richard Harris and Craig Challen for their work in Thailand in 2018. The headline read as follows: 'Bravery of selfless, dedicated Thai cave rescuers earns joint honour'. The article was about the rescue of 12 teenagers and their soccer coach who were trapped by floodwaters in an underground river system, and about the two Australian cave divers who played a vital role

---

15 Hooven, *Testosterone*, p 253.
16 Hooven, *Testosterone*, p 260.

in that rescue. For their courage, skill and self-sacrifice, they had been jointly awarded 'Australian of the Year'.[17]

But just underneath that story sat a second and equally prominent headline: 'Alcoholic squatter arrested over Aiia'. Codey Herrmann, a 20-year-old would-be rap artist, had been charged with the rape and murder of 21-year-old exchange student Aiia Maasarwe in Bundoora, Melbourne. Next to the article was a chilling picture he had posted of himself on Facebook—half smiling, with glassy teddy-bear eyes and a can of Jack Daniels in his hand—just hours after he'd killed Aiia. Our nation mourned over this senseless crime. The story told of how Aiia's father had planned a trip from Israel to Australia to visit his daughter, a journey he now had to make with a broken heart.

Together, these two articles vividly illustrate the best and the worst men can be. How we make sense of them—the narrative we find most compelling—will depend on our worldview and our perception of masculinity. Some of us will want to emphasize the strong, protective and competent male; others will see confirmation that all men are potential predators. Perhaps we should see that men are capable of both of these extremes.

A few pages from now, we'll look at the label 'toxic masculinity' and the understandable but wrong response, which is to weaken or dilute concepts of masculinity within our culture. Here's the irony, though: weakness is actually the source of the problem with masculinity. Ask yourself: In the newspaper stories above, who is the strong man and who is the weak one? To quote Canadian psychologist Jordan Peterson, "If you think tough men are dangerous, wait until you see what weak men are capable of".[18] The big or physically strong man who is aggressive or

---

17 This event has now been made into a movie, *Thirteen Lives* (2022), directed by Ron Howard and starring Viggo Mortensen, Colin Farrell and Joel Edgerton.
18 JB Peterson, *12 Rules for Life: An antidote to chaos*, Penguin Books, 2018, p 332.

intimidates other people, the man who throws his weight around, is actually a very weak man where it really matters: in heart and character. Men become dangerous not because their masculinity is toxic but because their *humanity* is. These men lack the sense of purpose and the moral framework that show them how to use their strength well.

In short, the answer is not to weaken men, but to help them grow stronger.

But before we throw ourselves into that touchy subject, let's look at how the definition of masculinity has changed in recent times.

The wrong sort of masculinity

There are plenty of wrong definitions of masculinity. Sometimes it's measured by how much grog a bloke can drink, or how many 'f-bombs' he can fit into a sentence.[19] A generation ago, tattoos were seen as the mark of true masculinity. But these days there are more tatts on show in a young mums' playgroup than at a bikie convention. Physical size and strength have also been up there as marks of a 'real man', but are they really reliable markers of masculinity? I've known big men with little hearts, and small men who are giants in terms of courage and character.

Joe Ehrmann is a champion American football player. He was and still is a big dude: 1.93 m and 115 kg (6′ 4″, 250 lb). He played in the NFL for 14 years and he's now around 70 years old. In a book inspired by his career, *Season of Life*, he speaks about the myths that men begin imbibing from as early as seven years of age, including the following components of what he calls a "false masculinity":

1. athletic ability that highlights size and strength
2. sexuality that uses women to gratify personal needs

19 'Grog' is Australian slang for alcohol.

3. economic success where self-worth is equated with net worth.[20]

Mr Ehrmann is exactly right. As I said above, I've known men who are big and strong and yet had hearts the size of a pea. A man who uses size and strength to intimidate other people is a very small man indeed. Further, all the sexual 'conquests' in the world are not worth comparing to the intimacy a man creates when he keeps his lifelong promise to be faithful and intimate with just one woman. And, ironically, the man who measures himself by the size of his bank balance will never have enough money to seem big in his own eyes.

So if that's false masculinity, how are we to properly understand true or healthy masculinity? And why does the quest to do so often feel like it's being undervalued?

Our culture has changed dramatically in my lifetime, and many of those changes were undoubtedly needed. Attitudes towards women and the opportunities they are afforded needed drastic revision. Thankfully, we've seen some gains. I have three daughters who have been able to pursue whatever career they chose and had the ability to undertake. I realize I'm a proud dad so I won't bore you by going on about it, but my girls have all done well in the areas they have chosen. They have grown up in an age which has increasingly aimed to redress the gender imbalance, and they have benefited accordingly. There's a whole range of things we take for granted now that were not open to my mum's generation, such as access for women to tertiary education, bank loans not needing to be in a husband's name, equal pay for equal work, and even a whole range of sporting options. We still have a way to go in all this, but real progress has been made.

Feminism as a cultural and political movement has been the

---

20 J Marx, *Season of Life: A football star, a boy, a journey to manhood*, Simon & Schuster, 2004, pp 35-36, 71-73.

engine that has powered many of these gains. But the advocacy of women's rights on the basis of the equality of the sexes has also ushered in some changes that have not been quite so beneficial. For example, the narrative that "You can have it all!"—a stellar career, a deep and satisfying marriage, children (and quality time to nurture them), *and* sleep—has made for a generation of very tired people. (Inevitably, this is affecting women disproportionately, because too often men are abdicating their share of family duties and women are having to pick up the difference while also working in a paid job outside the home.) Sadly, increased freedom and independence for women has meant a diminishing of men's sense of obligation to care for and commit to their partners. The vast majority of single parents are women, who are much more likely to live in poverty.[21] I'm not criticizing the single mums at all; I'm just saying I think they've ended up with the rough end of the pineapple. It's very tough to raise kids on your own.

It seems to me that some women's rights advocates in recent times have seen gender 'equalization' as a zero-sum game—that is, in order to lift women up, you need to pull men down. Certainly in popular culture, in a slow death by a thousand cuts, the masculine 'brand' has been steadily undermined and trashed. Unhealthy representations of masculinity have crept more and more into books, songs, movies, television shows, podcasts and more. To take just one example, look at something as mundane as the television sitcom dad. Let me show you in seven TV shows how things have changed over the past fifty years, to highlight the downhill trend in how men are presented.

The Brady Bunch was a popular TV show, originally airing from 1969 to 1974, about the perfect blended family. The dad, Mike Brady, has his faults: he wears flares and has his hair

---

21 A Sebastian and I Ziv, *One in eight families: Australian single mothers' lives revealed*, Council of Single Mothers and their Children, 2019, accessed 7 January 2022 (csmc.org.au/publications/national-survey).

permed in the final season. But it was the 70s; we can forgive him. More importantly, Mr Brady is engaged with his family. He is the wise go-to man who is ultimately charged with sorting out the problems in his family's life.

Another positive father role model from the same time period was Howard Cunningham of *Happy Days*. He loves his family and is an ever-present source of stability in the weekly chaos created by Richie and the Fonz. Howard is the non-anxious, wise presence that the family needs.

It only takes a handful of years, though, for things to take a downward turn. In 1987, Al Bundy made his debut in our living rooms. *Married with Children* introduced us to a husband who is, not to put too fine a point on it, a useless slob. Then, only two years later, Homer Simpson arrived with the first episode of *The Simpsons*. Homer is well meaning and at least tries to engage with his family—but, let's be honest, he is entirely clueless. To quote Leonard Sax again:

> [Homer] is always an idiot, reliably a klutz, consistently the least intelligent character in any episode, with the possible exception of his son, Bart, or the family dog. By contrast, Homer's wife, Marge, is generally practical, although sometimes silly. The most intelligent character is usually the daughter Lisa, who routinely ignores her father's advice, because his advice is often hysterically awful.[22]

In most of the more than 700 episodes so far, it's fair to say Homer is usually part of the problem rather than part of the solution.

The next man to take the prominent TV-dad baton is Raymond Barone from *Everybody Loves Raymond* (1996-2005). Once again, the male character is thoughtless, stupid and useless. Jour-

22 L Sax, *Boys Adrift: The five factors driving the growing epidemic of unmotivated boys and underachieving young men*, Basic Books, 2007, p 221.

nalist Alison Cameron nails it when she describes the lazy male stereotyping:

> [Ray] is a thoughtless husband and a poor father interested only in television, food and sex. Cue laughter.
>
> He is a stereotyped manchild who spends much of his time trying to shirk his responsibilities.
>
> In one show while trying to extricate himself from some parental duties he says to his wife: "You're so great with the kids, you know what to do. If it were up to me they'd be eating cereal for dinner and wearing the boxes."[23]

It seems not everybody loves Raymond, though it has certainly been a popular show.

By the time we reach 2003, with the advent of *Family Guy*, things have become much worse. Peter Griffin, the head of this particular family, is basically Homer Simpson without any of his redeeming qualities. The result is a totally useless human being ... er, animated character.

Present-day productions haven't relented on the man-brand trashing. Consider the impression of fatherhood we get from *Peppa Pig*. Enormously popular with little kids, this highly successful show has a particular way of portraying Daddy Pig. Surprise, surprise, it's not pretty, as is so eloquently pointed out in *Esquire Magazine*:

> Daddy Pig is a bespectacled pink blob with a booming voice and bum-fluff whiskers.
>
> An unqualified disaster when it comes to map reading, DIY and barbecues, three of the skills men might traditionally expect to possess, his favourite pastimes are lying on

---

23 A Cameron, 'Everybody loves lazy stereotyping of male roles', *The Sydney Morning Herald*, 11 April 2005, accessed 7 January 2022 (smh.com.au/national/everybody-loves-lazy-stereotyping-of-male-roles-20050411-gdl3r0.html).

the sofa watching television, sitting in the sun reading a newspaper and eating vast quantities of chocolate cake.[24]

Clearly the well-worn cliché of male uselessness is alive and well. What makes this myopic swine different from his bumbling cartoon father predecessors, though, is that he appears in a format aimed squarely at children aged 2-5. Such examples have led Kathleen Parker, author of *Save the Males*, to ask:

> What message are [children] absorbing today when nearly every TV father is either absent or absurd? Or when children are always smarter and wiser than the old man? Not to exaggerate the influence of a single show or episode, but over time, negative stereotyping is absorbed into the culture, and the message is that men are not only bad, they're stupid and unreliable.[25]

So there you have it: a short history of the television sitcom dad's downward spiral. Now, I'm aware that this trend has its outliers. Archie Bunker (*All in the Family*, 1971-1979) was a racist bigot and pig-headed husband fifty years ago; and the much more recent Australian children's show *Bluey* portrays a dad who is both wise and engaged. But my overall point is to show the clear trend in how men, and particularly dads, are portrayed on TV.

And television is not the only culprit; it's just the most obvious one. When my kids were young, I'd read stories to them each night. One series I picked up was called *The Berenstain Bears*—a series of clever, nicely illustrated stories that deliver plenty of laughs. Look closely, though, and you'll notice that the dad is the fool at the centre of most of the jokes. He's like one of the kids, or

---

24 D Davies, 'What Peppa Pig tells us about British fatherhood', *Esquire*, 17 June 2014, accessed 7 January 2022 (esquire.com/uk/culture/news/a6519/has-peppa-pig-got-fatherhood-spot-on).

25 K Parker, *Save the Males: Why men matter; why women should care*, Random House, 2010, p 18.

worse, and regularly part of the problem rather than the solution. It's usually the mum who has to save the day and cover up for her husband's stupidity. Eventually I stopped reading these books to my kids. I may not be the sharpest tool in the shed, but I'm smart enough to realize it's not a good idea to read books to your children that teach them dads are idiots. Of course, there are exceptions to every rule, but popular culture very often presents men and fathers as incompetent fools.

And things get even worse when masculinity itself is attacked as being 'toxic'.

2. MASCULINITY: UNDER ATTACK

THERE'S NO DENYING IT: there are times when men behave very badly. Take, for example, news columnist Jill Stark's experience at the football in Melbourne one night. Having been to a concert next door to the MCG, the iconic stadium where tens of thousands of people had just attended an AFL game, Jill describes the fear and loneliness that engulfed her as she waited for a ride home, facing harassment from multiple different groups of men:

> There were catcalls and abuse, a demand to "smile, love", and pointed questions about where I was going and who I was waiting for.
>
> As I tried to make myself smaller—as if by bowing my head and hunching my shoulders I would be less visible—a guy hung out of a car window yelling obscenities in my direction while the driver beeped his horn.
>
> I stood there in tears—a woman alone in the dark just wanting to get home—wishing it would stop. Wishing someone would intervene. And thinking of all the women who never made it home safe.[1]

---

1   J Stark, 'Groups of men harassed me to tears in the street—and no one acted', *The Sydney Morning Herald*, 26 March 2019, accessed 7 January 2022 (smh.com.au/lifestyle/gender/groups-of-guys-harassed-me-to-tears-in-the-street-and-no-one-acted-20190325-p517g6.html).

This is blatant sexual harassment taking place in one of Australia's capital cities in the middle of huge crowds of people. What is going on?

Sadly, media reports like this one are all too common. We see it in sport, where our headlines regularly document the abuse of women by high-profile sportsmen (the latest variety being the posting of sex videos without the woman's consent). We see it in politics, where the culture of Australia's entire federal parliament has recently been placed under the spotlight after a spate of sexual assault allegations prompted thousands to attend rallies across the country to protest against the sexual abuse of women.[2] And we see it in the home—domestic violence against women persists as a widespread problem in our society. The fact that we need a White Ribbon Day to demonstrate that we stand against domestic violence shows the size and scope of the problem. Of course domestic violence is wrong—we shouldn't need to be convinced of this, and we certainly shouldn't need to be told to actually do something about it! And yet it continues to be a huge problem.

Given these obvious realities, it is perhaps easy to see why the idea of masculinity is so often under attack in our culture.

But while I do not want to minimize or excuse *any* bad behaviour from men, I do want to suggest that the underlying problem isn't masculinity itself, and so the attack on masculinity is misplaced.

Let's briefly look at three different aspects of the current attack on masculinity, before we think about healthy masculinity and why it is valuable.

---

2   S Khalil, 'Australia March 4 Justice: Thousands march against sexual assault', *BBC News*, 15 March 2021, accessed 7 January 2022 (bbc.com/news/world-australia-56397170).

Attack 1: All masculinity is toxic

The label 'toxic masculinity' is thrown around regularly in the gender wars, but is rarely defined. So let's have a go at doing just that. The top definition in the online *Urban Dictionary* says that 'toxic masculinity' is:

> A social science term that describes narrow repressive type [*sic*] of ideas about the male gender role, that defines masculinity as exaggerated masculine traits like being violent, unemotional, sexually aggressive, and so forth. Also suggests that men who act too emotional or maybe aren't violent enough or don't do all of the things that "real men" do, can get their "man card" taken away.[3]

So that's one definition. But let's see what one of Australia's leading feminists thinks. In her book *Boys Will Be Boys*, Clementine Ford uses the term so frequently that you begin to wonder if she believes there is any other kind of masculinity. Ford is a clear communicator and a gifted writer, and there's no shortage of energy in the book. She's often angry and a bit 'shouty', but I can understand and sympathize with a surprising amount of what she has to say. Here is her slightly colourful description of toxic masculinity:

> An inability to 'deal with emotions in healthy ways' is what toxic masculinity is all about. And, in most cases, what this really stems from is fear. They're afraid of the world changing, because then they might have to actually work a bit harder to be seen as important within it. So they [s---] on women and people of colour and anyone else fighting for political equality alongside them and screech about 'SJWs'

---

3   SparklyNinja, 'Toxic masculinity', *Urban Dictionary*, 12 November 2017, accessed 7 January 2022 (urbandictionary.com/define.php?term=Toxic%20Masculinity).

and feminism being 'cancer' and think this is enough to mask the stench of fear that rolls off them in waves. But as any true fan of *Star Wars* can tell you, fear is the path to the dark side. Fear leads to anger. Anger leads to hate. Hate leads to suffering.[4]

It may be a little ironic that Clementine Ford seems pretty angry as she insists that anger is a huge part of the problem, but I don't blame her for being angry. I can certainly see why many women are angry. But I'm not sure that serving up blanket condemnation with little attempt at understanding does any good. Of course, neither does a bunch of angry men pushing men's rights. Both extremes generate heat but no light.

Here's my argument: when men behave badly, it isn't their masculinity that's toxic; it's their *humanity*. The decision to abuse power in order to control or humiliate another person, the refusal to demonstrate compassion—those are problems with their humanity. What our world needs is the sort of men Jill Stark would have liked to meet on that footpath outside the MCG. We need men who are not *less* masculine, but who are *properly* masculine; the sort of men who will step up to protect the vulnerable. (And women *are* vulnerable. I know Lara Croft, Captain Marvel and many other similar heroines would have us believe otherwise, but women remain vulnerable to men in many ways, especially when it comes to harassment and violence. It's why we have White Ribbon Day.)

If you know anything about Jesus, do you think he would have watched a woman being harassed or humiliated and done nothing? Not a chance. In fact, history records him protecting women who were the sex workers of his day (Luke 7:36-50). He also prevented the abuse of a woman caught in adultery (John 8:2-11). He

4 Ford, *Boys Will Be Boys*, p 98.

didn't approve of the women's behaviour, but he would not let men mistreat them.

There are men in this world who protect women like Jesus did. It's true that too often we read about men misusing their power to intimidate, or worse, but there are also stories about men who get it right. Here's one example: in 2020, a man named Mark Rapley heroically jumped onto a great white shark and punched it repeatedly when it tried to maul his wife, Chantelle Doyle:

> "It was unbelievable, the scream was incredible and there was splashing everywhere," witness Jed Toohey told the *Daily Telegraph*.
>
> "Mark was a hero. He started laying into the shark because it wouldn't let go."[5]

Along with the article itself, some of the comments on Mark's heroics made for very interesting reading:

> Eli 101: Taking one's vows seriously. Well done, Mark.

> Elizabeth: This is what nearly all men would do for women. Let's stop the appalling assault on the male sex with labels such as toxic masculinity for one.

Reading stories like this makes it crystal clear what real, healthy masculinity looks like. I don't know if I'd be able to think as clearly in extreme circumstances like this. I hope I'd be able to do the right thing. But surely we can all agree that this is the ideal we want to strive for. And what's that ideal? It's manning up when you see that someone needs looking after. Speaking up. Stepping up. Doing whatever you can to protect and help someone who needs you. It might mean saying something when a

---

5   C Kellett, 'Husband punches shark after wife attacked near Port Macquarie on NSW coast', *The Australian*, 16 August 2020, accessed 6 November 2021 (theaustralian.com.au/nation/husband-punches-shark-after-wife-attacked-near-port-macquarie-on-nsw-coast/news-story/0fae1f75c25d3dd045baaa535d784853).

bunch of clowns are harassing a woman. Or it could be something as simple as offering to walk a woman to her car at night. Your offer might be casually dismissed and you may feel like an idiot for offering—but take the chance. Feeling like an idiot won't kill you, and the offer may be much more appreciated than you expect. Either way, it's the right thing to do.

I know we're not all Mark Rapley, but it's worth determining before an incident what you would do. That way, you're ready to do it if and when the time comes. Tell yourself, "I will stand up or speak up, or step up for the vulnerable and for those who need help". That might be a woman or a child or an older person, or a guy who's struggling. It might involve something as simple as offering to help the young mum with two kids and a pram get on or off a bus.

But no matter how you're called to act, don't let the 'toxic masculinity' label deter you from doing what's good and right. True masculinity is not toxic; instead, it's about stepping up to protect or help those who need it.

Attack 2: Patriarchy is evil

The problems for men and masculinity only get bigger when critics attempt to forge a link between patriarchy and many of the world's worst evils. For these critics, the term 'patriarchy' describes a system where men hold all the power by virtue of the social and political positions they hold. Author and professor Robert Jensen says patriarchy is:

> ... a system that delivers material benefits to men—unequally depending on men's other attributes (such as race, class, sexual orientation, nationality, immigration status) and on men's willingness to adapt to patriarchal values—but patriarchy constrains all women.[6]

6   R Jensen, *The End of Patriarchy: Radical feminism for men*, Spinifex Press, 2017, p 59.

Notice those last four words: "patriarchy constrains *all women*". Clementine Ford would surely agree, seeing patriarchy as the source of practically all our griefs:

> The patriarchal system under which we all labour is designed to uphold this power while punishing those who challenge its existence in any way. Within this structure, boys are given the space to unfurl and grow, to creep further and further outwards, while girls are forced to retreat ever more inwards.[7]

What Ford is claiming in the quote above simply does not fit the facts. As an example, the reality is that boys are slipping further and further behind in terms of educational achievements in the Western world. Study after study reports the increasing numbers of under-achieving and disengaged boys in education systems that favour girls.[8] Young men are under-represented in Australian university enrolments, with women accounting for 58 percent of all students in 2016.[9] The proportion of female postgraduates is even higher. To briefly consider one other issue, what about the area of mental health? In 2019, 3,318 Australians took their own lives; three quarters of these people were male.[10]

What's more, the negative side of patriarchy is only one part of the story. I know men have misused power in the past, but they have also died as soldiers or worked themselves to death to provide for their families.

I also realize that we haven't yet arrived at complete gender equality—women are still discriminated against or held back in some areas—but to claim that "patriarchy constrains all women" or that "girls are forced to retreat ever more inwards" in the

7   Ford, *Boys Will Be Boys*, p 8.
8   See Sax, *Boys Adrift*; and Farrell and Gray, *The Boy Crisis*.
9   Larkins, *Male students remain underrepresented in Australian universities. Should we be concerned?*.
10 Lifeline, *Data and statistics*, Lifeline website, n.d., accessed 7 January 2022 (lifeline.org.au/resources/data-and-statistics).

modern world is patently nonsense. To take just one example, as of late 2021 there were 27 female heads of state in countries as diverse as Bangladesh, Singapore, Greece and Ethiopia.[11]

My point is simply this: not *all* women are being constrained. The claims made by Jensen, by Ford, and by so many others today are exaggerated and therefore confusing, perhaps even dangerous. The potential to reach the highest offices in the land is there and is being exercised; girls are outpacing boys in many key educational and social measures.

And yet more change is obviously still needed. The question is: *How much* change is needed?

The problem for many begins with the very concept of 'hierarchy' being seen as wicked. If you believe that a 'flat' organization of society is the only way to promote flourishing, then hierarchy is always going to be considered an evil, especially as it relates to men being in the positions of power. In the eyes of people like Robert Jensen, patriarchy 'normalizes' hierarchy because masculinity is always about women being dominated. Therefore, if you're going to solve the perceived problem of patriarchy, you must begin by getting rid of hierarchies "... unless a compelling argument can be made that the hierarchy is necessary to help those with less power in the system, a test that can rarely be met".[12] Here is the worldview that all of life is a struggle for power. In this view, all hierarchies must be inconsistent with human flourishing, because they must always be about dominating or suppressing other people. So if we can just do away with all hierarchies, with all authority, then society will be better off.

This is not just unlivable, but also really dumb. There will always be hierarchies in human relationships, though that does

---

11 Wikipedia, 'List of elected and appointed female heads of state and government', *Wikipedia*, 4 January 2022, accessed 11 January 2022 (en.wikipedia.org/wiki/List_of_elected_and_appointed_female_heads_of_state_and_government).

12 Jensen, *The End of Patriarchy*, p 60.

not always mean there will be domination.

Let me illustrate. My wife, Kathy, is a brilliant cook. People are often asking her how to cook different dishes, or how to show hospitality to large groups. In the ranks of the hospitable, Kathy is high up in the hierarchy. But this is hardly about dominance or oppression. It's simply about competence or a talent for service— perhaps even about love in action. And that's why people seek her out. When we want to find a builder, we do the same thing: we ask around for someone who is competent and trustworthy. This is even more important if you're looking for a surgeon.

Hierarchies are often necessary and are regularly built on competence, responsibility or service. They need not—in fact must not—be built on dominance or exploitation. Indeed, the cornerstone of the Christian faith is the lordship or authority of Jesus—the head of a hierarchy if ever there was one—and yet the lordship of Jesus is history's greatest example of love and sacrificial service. Jesus "did not come to be served, but to serve, and to give his life as a ransom for many" (Mark 10:45).[13]

Jesus calls those who follow him, both men and women, to model that attitude of sacrificial service.

Attack 3: Masculinity needs to be feminized

If masculinity is seen as harmful, then the obvious next step is to dilute it, if not do away with it altogether. But what should it be diluted with? Of course, masculinity is to some extent defined by culture, and there are different ways of appearing masculine. My

---

13 A quick word about Bible references throughout this book (in case you're not familiar with these kinds of references): when I say 'Mark 10:45', I mean the book of Mark, chapter 10 (the large numbers as printed in a Bible), verse 45 (the small numbers). Some of the biblical books I quote will be referred to with their abbreviated name (e.g. 'Gen' means 'Genesis'; 'Matt' means 'Matthew'). If you're in any doubt about which Bible book is being referred to, a quick check of the contents page in a Bible should make it pretty obvious.

patriarchs were given to eating haggis and chasing each other around Scotland with claymore swords while wearing tartan skirts—sorry, kilts. While reducing the overall amount of weaponry in society is by all accounts a positive move for societal wellbeing (i.e. for people not dying), another fundamental transformation seems to be taking place in our culture in recent years. I sense a move by some to not just *devalue* masculinity, but to domesticate men by removing anything and everything that marks them out as men. Many men seem to have given in to the cultural pressures and have been emasculated to the point of being feminized.

Consider Chanel's decision to jump onto this bandwagon by launching a makeup range for men. Its tagline: *Beauty knows no gender.*[14] Kathleen Parker, author of *Save the Males*, says it amounts to a deliberate feminizing of men so that they're basically unrecognizable *as men*:

> Obviously, concepts of manhood or masculinity shift with the times. Once upon a time, men in ruffled shirts and powdered wigs were considered wildly macho, and clearly men in skirts didn't start last year in Milan. The difference today is that fashions are intended to make men look or seem like women.[15]

Journalist Nikki Gemmell embraces this trend in her article 'Beta blokes are better':

> Feminine men, in my experience, are more confident and therefore comfortable with their sexuality ...
>
> Give me a man ... who's comfortable enough to wear nail polish. Because that speaks sexual confidence; nothing to

---

14 C Ollinger, 'Chanel expands luxe beauty's reach with "Boy de Chanel" collection', *PSFK*, 13 January 2020, accessed 7 January 2022 (psfk.com/2020/01/chanel-boy-de-chanel-collection.html).

15 Parker, *Save the Males*, p 109.

THE MANUAL

hide and nothing to be afraid of. Give me a playful man who never, entirely, grows up; who never clamps down into curmudgeonliness and grump. Give me a man comfortable enough to farewell his mates with "love you" and call them darling, which I've recently witnessed young heterosexual men do and it feels tender and gorgeous and confident.[16]

This sounds great fun, but does Nikki Gemmell really want a world full of playful men who never entirely grow up? A world full of Peter Pans? Really? I don't want to clamp down into curmudgeonliness (great word, by the way—it means something like 'being easily annoyed'), but I believe we need boys who really grow up into men. It's the grown-ups (men and women) who turn up at their jobs each day and make our world work, who raise families and pay mortgages and do other boring stuff so that the people who depend on them can have a life. (I'll say more about the need for boys to become men in chapter 4.)

However, the commercial media continue to both reflect and promote Gemmell's viewpoint. Advertisers deliberately blur the lines between men and women. Very often, the line between the masculine and the feminine is so blurred it's hard to tell the gender of the model. Today's fashion industry enthusiastically embraces androgynous dressing:

Naturally, the vast evolution of our view on gender has trickled down into the fashion industry, causing designers to seriously consider for whom they make their clothes, and what this says about their brand. Though the change is slow to take hold in mass production, designers have begun to blur the lines between men's and women's fashion with the

---

16 N Gemmell, 'Beta blokes are better', *The Australian*, 19 May 2018, accessed 6 November 2021 (theaustralian.com.au/life/weekend-australian-magazine/beta-blokes-are-better/news-story/3c89756f3a4b5eed1df418a06956aad0).

introduction of androgynous pieces into their collections.[17]

Clementine Ford wants to go further and blur the lines between masculine and feminine behaviour. In her public letter to her young son she writes:

> Personally, I look forward to a future in which my son will be supported to wear what he likes without fear of being bullied, degraded or made to feel subhuman. Where the concept of boys wearing clothes commonly deemed feminine won't even be a source of amusement or embarrassment anymore because society will have grown up enough to recognise that there is nothing embarrassing about being a girl.[18]

Clementine can, of course, raise her son how she chooses, but since she has offered this in a public letter, it seems fair and reasonable to make a polite comment. I too want a society where people are not bullied. I mean it: I hate bullying with a passion. Unfortunately, there's not a snowball's chance that society will become like that, in my lifetime or her son's. I don't say that lightly. Tragically, there's something wrong in many human hearts that leads to the misuse of power and the belittling and intimidation of the weak. It's just further evidence of the default setting of selfishness inside us.

This means, for one thing, we need to raise kids to be strong, rather than over-protected. (I realize this is politically incorrect, and I offer this as a personal view.) Unfortunately, often the best answer to stop a boy being bullied is to teach him how to defend himself. A boy who is responsibly taught to defend himself and others is not only a curb to bullies, but is simultaneously more

---

17 B Schneider, 'Blurring the line between men's and women's fashion', *Fashion Mannuscript*, 1 February 2019, accessed 6 November 2021 (www.mann publications.com/fashionmannuscript/2019/02/01/blurring-the-line-between-mens-and-womens-fashion).

18 Ford, *Boys Will Be Boys*, p 38.

aware of his innate strength and therefore less likely to abuse it. There are many different options now—various martial arts, for example—that will teach boys (and girls) self-confidence, discipline, fitness and self-defence.

But more to the point, Ford's claim is fundamentally flawed. The idea that her son being able to wear a dress would be evidence that "society will have grown up enough to recognize that there is nothing embarrassing about being a girl" is nonsense. Of course, there's nothing embarrassing about being a girl at all. But her son isn't a girl! Raising her son to look and act like someone he's not isn't doing him any favours. Boys should be kind, gentle and loving, absolutely. But the real world is tough and, whoever he becomes, he will need to be able to stand up for himself, what he believes, and the people he loves. Twirling in dresses and sparkly shoes is likely to make him a target. I wish it wasn't the case, but reality often doesn't give us what we wish for. Seeking to feminize men to the point that they lose all the distinctives of their gender flows from the assumption that masculinity is not just culturally unnecessary but somehow wicked or evil. As we've seen, when men demonstrate their strengths, it's denounced as either toxic or as evidence of an oppressive patriarchy.

How did we get here? It's more than just the general softening of our society—although our first-world culture is now so comfortable that it inevitably softens some men. I think there are two related answers.

The first and most obvious answer is that some women are afraid of men and view them as potential predators. One proposed answer to that problem is to declaw men—emasculate and feminize them.

About 15 years ago, our family had a Staffordshire Terrier named Barney. Every member of the family loved him, especially my teenage son, for whom Barney was like a little brother. Barney was fully wired for every activity. In the end, it was his desire to chase the ladies that had him escape from our yard and be run over by a bus. Broken hearts all round—especially my son's. As a consequence, when I wanted to get another Staffordshire, the only way I could get the motion passed in 'the senate' at home was to agree that we would have the new staffy's 'batteries' disconnected. So Musket (our new dog) was off to the vet when he was a few months old. That procedure has made him much easier to handle, much more obedient, and happy to just lie asleep in the sun a lot of the time. He's a good dog, but not as headstrong or adventurous as Barney.

I wonder if this idea of having one's batteries disconnected is—in a purely metaphorical way, of course—what's happening to many of our young men now. Are men perceived to be safer the less masculine they are? If that's the case, it's a tragedy, because healthy masculinity in a man should create the exact opposite feelings in the people around him. I'll come back to this in the next chapter.

The second answer is somewhat related. The feminist narrative is built around power—wresting power from men and from the patriarchy that holds back women. The way to achieve this is not simply to make women stronger, but to make men as weak as possible. And surely gender-neutral 'men' must be safer than masculine men.

In the next chapter, I'll argue that the opposite is true *if* men live out a healthy masculinity. The more men who will sacrificially love and care for those around them, the safer our society will be for everyone, especially the vulnerable. The man who has a healthy masculinity is concerned to care for others. The man who understands his masculinity and uses it to serve others is stronger in many ways, and the people who know him—especially the women in his life—rejoice in this. Why? The truly masculine man makes the people around him feel safe. Things are more stable because he's around. They know he's committed to caring for them in whatever way is needed, however he can.

I'll come back to this point at the end of the chapter.

So, having grappled with three of the most common ways in which masculinity is under attack in our culture today, let's turn to think about why masculinity still matters, how we should rightly understand it, and why we should still value it.

Masculinity: Why it matters

David D Gilmore was professor of anthropology at State University in New York in 1990 when he wrote *Manhood in the Making*. Professor Gilmore researched masculinity across a wide range of cultures, including the European Western world, Africa, Asia, the Pacific Islands, and many other traditional societies. In his study, he identified many similarities shared by the vast majority of societies. In almost all of these places, it *cost* the individual something to become a man. There were initiations that made it significant—costly—to move from being a boy to being a man. Gilmore ponders the existence of an archetype or 'deep structure' to masculinity, and asks:

> What explains all these similarities? Why the trials, and the testing and the seemingly gratuitous agonies of man-playing? Why is so much indoctrination and motivation needed in all these cultures to make real men?[19]

His conclusion is that men need to step up and do hard things: "The harsher the environment and the scarcer the resources, the more manhood is stressed as an inspiration and a goal".[20] In short, Gilmore says that boys need their strength to be tested in order to become men.

The more we trash masculinity in the eyes of boys, the more

19 D Gilmore, *Manhood in the Making: Cultural concepts of masculinity*, Yale University Press, 1990, p 20.
20 Gilmore, *Manhood in the Making*, p 224.

we remove the inspiration to become strong men, the sort of men who rise above their circumstances. Instead, our cultural devaluation of manhood is beginning to result in psychologically lost, weak and disengaged boys.[21]

Leonard Sax speaks extensively about this disconnection in his book *Boys Adrift*. He discusses the huge number of American boys who have become disengaged from real life. His list of contributing factors includes a school system that by design favours girls, a massive rise in the diagnosis and medicating of ADHD among boys, a social retreat into online pastimes such as video games, and the resulting "failure to launch" into adult life.[22] His findings are corroborated by Philip Zimbardo and Nikita Coulombe in their book *Man Disconnected*, where they write about the huge numbers of boys who are addicted to video games and pornography, who suffer from obesity, and who have withdrawn from real-world relationships.[23]

Why does all of this matter so much? Gilmore's research into masculinity has led him to conclude: "Manhood is the social barrier that societies must erect against entropy, human enemies, the forces of nature, time, and all the human weaknesses that endanger group life".[24] I suppose it's possible that Western societies are reinventing themselves so that there will no longer be any need for men to step up and lead, love, care, protect and provide as they have done in every other culture known in history; "It's tough to make predictions, especially about the future".[25] So yes, it's possible; but I very much doubt it. I fear that Western cultures

---

21 See Farrell and Gray, *The Boy Crisis*; Sax, *Boys Adrift*; and P Zimbardo and ND Coulombe, *Man Disconnected: How technology has sabotaged what it means to be male*, Rider Books, 2015.

22 Leonard Sax deals with each of these factors at length in chapters 2-6 of *Boys Adrift*.

23 Zimbardo and Coulombe, *Man Disconnected*.

24 Gilmore, *Manhood in the Making*, p 226.

25 This saying is attributed to Yogi Berra, a professional baseballer in the 1940s, 1950s and 1960s.

are in for a world of pain in future generations as we uncover the consequences of dismantling masculinity. As the French philosopher Voltaire put it, "History is filled with the sound of silken slippers going downstairs and wooden shoes coming up".

I can't see exactly where the wooden shoes will have to climb from, but our society is currently making its descent in silken slippers. There is no widespread alarm about the loss of strong masculinity, only a relaxed acceptance. Yet a society that doesn't value healthy masculinity will lose many of the qualities that guarantee its stability. As we've seen in this chapter, it's already happening.

We need to end the gender war. We need to end the push to label masculinity—something that has historically and multiculturally been seen as good, natural and important—as toxic. We need to encourage the development of men who will take responsibility for the people around them; men who will act responsibly as husbands, fathers, sons, colleagues and leaders. We need males who are inspired to be men, not large boys. We need men to live with a healthy masculinity.

Masculinity: Understanding it

But what exactly is masculinity, and how does it relate to being a male? Or how does femininity relate to being a female? Masculinity and femininity can be hard to define. For example, Alan Medinger, the author of *Growth into Manhood*, says that explaining masculinity on its own becomes circular: "Masculine means having the qualities found especially in men. Men are those creatures who have masculine qualities."[26] He rightly points out that masculinity needs to be understood in relationship with femi-

---

26 A Medinger, *Growth into Manhood: Resuming the journey*, Waterbrook Press, 2000, p 82.

ninity. The masculine and feminine exist on a series of continuums. Men and women will exhibit more masculine or more feminine character traits along these scales.

Here are four continuums Medinger suggests for understanding masculine and feminine traits:

a. Outer-directed vs inner-directed

The masculine faces the world: It is oriented to things; it explores; it climbs. Its energy is directed towards the physical: measuring, moving, building, conquering. The feminine looks inward toward feeling, sensing, knowing in the deepest sense. Its energy is directed toward relationships, coming together, nurturing, helping. ... In fact, another way to describe this same contrast is masculine *doing* and feminine *being*.[27]

b. Initiation vs response

It is the masculine part of us that decides to start a new project, move to a new country, initiate marriage. The feminine will be the helper, the encourager, the supporter of another's plan or dream. The masculine loves to try new things; the feminine takes joy in helping and serving. The masculine proposes; the feminine accepts.[28]

c. Leadership vs cohesion

The masculine is about taking authority and leadership, the feminine is the power to hold things together. For example, the masculine may be the head of the house taking leadership, but it is the feminine that will hold the family and relationships together. So often in families it's mum who holds people and relationships together.[29]

27 Medinger, *Growth into Manhood*, p 84.
28 Medinger, *Growth into Manhood*, p 85.
29 Medinger, *Growth into Manhood*, pp 85-86.

d. Truth vs mercy

The masculine seeks truth; the feminine, mercy. The masculine operates on principle; the feminine is moved by compassion. The masculine looks to the long term good; the feminine looks at the immediate human need. The masculine has a passion for truth, the feminine for love.[30]

Notice that Medinger is not saying all men are one way and all women are another, as he explains:

What I have described is a cluster of attributes that we have defined as masculine: the capacity to initiate, an outer directedness, the ability to exercise authority or make decisions, and a passion for truth—all related to one another with the common thread of masculine *doing*. And we also have a cluster of attributes that we have defined as feminine: the capacity to respond, an inner directedness, the power that gives and sustains life, and a strong predilection toward love or mercy—all tied together with the common thread of feminine *being*. ... The masculine and feminine are of God, and therefore both are very good. ... Every person, male and female, embodies the masculine and the feminine. By God's design the masculine should be predominant in the man, and the feminine in the woman.[31]

This is crucial in helping us understand that there are no absolutes when it comes to what counts as 'masculine' and what counts as 'feminine'; each person has parts of both. And while there are only two sexes (and both sexes are good), each person is on a continuum of what we recognize as masculine traits and feminine traits. As Medinger says, "The masculine predominates in men; the feminine in women". Of course, the ways of showing

---

30 Medinger, *Growth into Manhood*, pp 86-87.
31 Medinger, *Growth into Manhood*, p 88.

masculinity and femininity will vary enormously from culture to culture in multiple ways—such as how people dress, how their hair is styled, and who they hold hands with.

Masculinity: Valuing it

We've seen that masculinity is not about size or athletic ability, nor is it about 'success' with the ladies or how much cash you have. In his excellent book *The New Manhood*, Steve Biddulph speaks about masculinity as the deliberate investment in the lives of those around us.[32] He tells of Australian Indigenous leader David Mowaljarlai, who "taught young men both black and white throughout his life. The culmination of his ceremonies was an initiatory message, and he stated it plainly: you are in this world to nurture and protect life. That is what men are for."[33] To nurture and protect life is a message that resonates with men. It's interesting that Jordan Peterson doesn't focus on young men—he's quite generic in the way he speaks—but his audiences around the world have been disproportionately filled with young men. They are the ones gravitating towards this message and embracing this call:

> It is for this reason that I tell my students: aim to be the person at your father's funeral that everyone, in their grief and misery, can rely on. There's a worthy and noble ambition: strength in the face of adversity. That is very different from the wish for a life free of trouble.[34]

32 Of course, women will invest in the lives of others as well, but they will tend to do this in ways that are different from men, as per Medinger's four continuums listed above.

33 S Biddulph, *The New Manhood: Love, freedom, spirit and the new masculinity*, Simon & Schuster, rev edn, 2019, p 184.

34 Peterson, *12 Rules for Life*, p 365.

Speaking of the one whom "everyone ... can rely on" inevitably reminds me of Jesus of Nazareth. In the ancient world, it was counterintuitive to believe that greatness could be found in the service of others, yet Jesus made this the very definition of greatness:

> Jesus called [the 12 disciples] together and said, "You know that those who are regarded as rulers of the Gentiles lord it over them, and their high officials exercise authority over them. Not so with you. Instead, whoever wants to become great among you must be your servant, and whoever wants to be first must be slave of all. For even the Son of Man[35] did not come to be served, but to serve, and to give his life as a ransom for many." (Mark 10:42-45)

Jesus' teaching and example have had a profound effect on the development of Western culture, and they continue to do so. In the last few years, multiple business leadership books have picked up this theme of 'servant leadership'. People are realizing that a commitment to serve others and put someone else's needs first will grow the lives of others and cause the right kind of organizational culture to prosper. By comparison, selfishness makes life shrink down or shrivel up. This is true in all walks of life, and especially in regard to our understanding of masculinity. Masculinity is fundamentally about *how* men use their power. When it is done in a healthy way, masculinity will serve and bless those it touches.

---

35 'Son of Man' is a title from the Old Testament that Jesus used to refer to himself.

3. MASCULINITY FROM THE MAKER'S MANUAL

NOW THAT WE have explored modern Western cultural per- spectives on gender, we can turn to the Bible's teaching on both gender differences and gender roles. The Bible sees the dif- ferences between the sexes as a good thing, and celebrates them. The sexes are created to be complementary rather than comba- tive. The creation of Eve is presented as God's kindness to Adam. The book of Genesis records the Creator's motive in the story itself as he observes that "It is not good for the man to be alone" (Gen 2:18). So she is made of the same flesh and blood as Adam, and yet Eve is different. They complement one another. God designs Eve not to be a *competer*, but to be a *completer* for the man—"a helper suitable for him", or literally "a help as opposite him" or "corresponding to him".[1] This doesn't diminish or demean her. In fact, the Hebrew word for helper (*āzar*) is often used to describe God.[2]

However, this pinnacle of the creation story is followed by a tragic sequence of events whereby the man and the woman reject

---

1 D Kidner, *Genesis*, Tyndale Old Testament Commentaries, IVP, Leicester, 1971, p 65.
2 The word *āzar* ('helper') is found particularly in the psalms. The Lord is seen as the helper of the underprivileged: the poor (Ps 72:12) and the fatherless (10:14; cf. Job 29:12). The psalmist confesses that he has no help but God (Ps 107:12-13). He is conscious of divine assistance at a time of suffering (28:7), at a time of oppression by enemies (54:4), and at a time of great personal distress (86:17).

God's rule and God's design. In Genesis 3, Adam and Eve believe the serpent's lie that God is holding out on them, and that they'll be better off if they make their own rules and disobey him. They choose to grasp at being gods themselves and, as a result, all human relationships—with God himself, with the creation around us, and with each other—are seriously damaged.

In the Genesis account, God says to Eve regarding Adam, "Your desire will be for your husband, and he will rule over you" (3:16). The same Hebrew word for desire is used a little later in Genesis to describe sin's desire to control Cain and lead him to become the first murderer.[3] In Eve's case, she will want to control Adam, and he will resist it. The marriage of the man and woman, which should have been characterized by mutual love, service and intimacy, now becomes a battleground in the making. As the old saying goes, he might aim to be the head of the marriage, but she will work at being the neck—moving the head in one way or the other.

The Bible's first man who didn't 'man up'

The Bible clearly presents men and women as equal before God, both created "in the image of God" (Gen 1:27). Both men and women are given the authority and the responsibility of ruling over (or caring for) the creation (1:28). Yet in Genesis 2, God gives Adam a particular responsibility to lead. The man is created first and placed in the garden, and God speaks to him about the only rule in the garden: namely, that God makes the rules, as symbolized by the commandment to not eat from the tree of the knowledge of good and evil (2:17). It is the man's responsibility to "leave his father and mother" and set up a new household with his wife (2:24). And when life is derailed by breaking the one

3 *Tshuwqah or teshurah* in Genesis 3:16 and 4:7.

commandment that God gave, Adam's major failing is his passivity. The Bible's account implies he was present when Eve spoke with the serpent; he just didn't have anything to say. I'm not sure what he was doing while he was standing there, but he certainly wasn't leading, caring and protecting. And so when God calls the first two humans to account, Adam is the first to be addressed, as he was primarily responsible (3:9-11). When Adam responds to God's question, he does so with a double buck-pass: "The woman you put here with me—she gave me some fruit from the tree, and I ate it" (v. 12). In essence, he tells God, "It's *her* fault, and it's *your* fault". This cowardly move doesn't exactly cover Adam in glory. In fact, later in the Bible this first great rebellion against God's authority is called 'the sin of Adam', not the sin of Eve (Rom 5:14).

The Genesis account packs so much explanatory power into so few sentences. The responsibility of men to lead is there for all to see in chapter 2, as is the male tendency to be passive and leave it to women to take the initiative in chapter 3. We see the damage that Adam's failure to take responsibility causes to all the relationships in Genesis—relationships with our Creator, with our work, with other people, and even with our spouses.

The rest of the Bible then goes on to show the consequences of Adam's sin and selfishness in the lives of every generation. We live with these consequences every day. Selfishness rules at a national, tribal, family, and personal level. So much pain in so many ways. We can see the consequences and feel the pain, and yet we can still feel that default setting of 'me first' deep within us. There's only ever been one person who lived the perfect, selfless life: Jesus shows us the perfect example of how to use love, strength and compassion.

The Bible's first man who did 'man up'

Canadian psychologist Jordan Peterson has a message that could be summarized like this: life is hard, so get your act together, pick up the heaviest burden you can carry, and start making life better for the people around you. You'd expect that this wouldn't be a great marketing success. But it's been truly fascinating to observe just how strongly this message has resonated with young men. In his book *12 Rules for Life,* Peterson notes the following in his seventh rule, "Pursue what is meaningful (not what is expedient)":

> Expedience is the following of blind impulse. It's short-term gain. It's narrow, and selfish. It lies to get its way. It takes nothing into account. It's immature and irresponsible. Meaning is its mature replacement. Meaning emerges when impulses are regulated, organized and unified. ... If you act properly your actions allow you to be psychologically integrated now, and tomorrow, and into the future, while you benefit yourself, your family, and the broader world around you.[4]

Long before Jordan Peterson hailed the benefits of selflessness, Jesus of Nazareth said this:

> "Whoever wants to be my disciple must deny themselves and take up their cross and follow me. For whoever wants to save their life will lose it, but whoever loses their life for me and for the gospel will save it." (Mark 8:34-35)

Jesus is the great example of how all people should use power. It's no surprise that what we see in Jesus is great power, used to care not for himself but for others. I've always thought you can tell the size of a man by the way he treats the little people who can do nothing for him, those that the world does not notice as it

---

4   Peterson, *12 Rules for Life,* p 199.

rushes past. On that test, Jesus is a giant. He has time for the poor, the crippled, the outcasts, men and women alike, regardless of rank or riches. In fact, in first-century Jewish culture the way Jesus treated women was indeed remarkable—so here are some remarks from writer Dorothy Sayers:

> They [women] had never known a man like this man—there never has been such another. A prophet and teacher who never nagged at them, never flattered or coaxed or patronized; who never made arch jokes about them, never treated them as either 'The women, God help us!' or 'The ladies, God bless them!'; who rebuked without querulousness and praised without condescension; who took their questions and arguments seriously; who never mapped out their sphere for them, never urged them to be feminine or jeered at them for being female; who had no axe to grind and no uneasy male dignity to defend; who took them as he found them and was completely unself-conscious. There is no act, no sermon, no parable in the whole Gospel that borrows its pungency from female perversity; nobody could possibly guess from the words and deeds of Jesus that there was anything 'funny' about woman's nature.[5]

But Jesus did more than simply demonstrate how to treat people well. Jesus came to die. He came to lay down his life for others.

Men need to know how to die. That is, they need to know how to lay down their lives for others. It's completely counterintuitive, but Jesus says we (men and women) will actually find life as we give our lives in the service of others. Throughout history, and until fairly recently, this had to happen quite literally: men

---

5   D Sayers, *Are Women Human? Penetrating, sensible, and witty essays on the role of women in society,* Downers Grove, 1971, p 47; quoted in ST Foh, *Women and the Word of God: A response to biblical feminism,* Presbyterian and Reformed Publishing, 1979, p 90.

needed to either die defending family, tribe or nation, or physically work themselves to death to feed and house their families. In our modern Western world, the need for this type of physical protection has almost disappeared. Many men still work hard physically, but not in the health-destroying ways of a century ago.

So we may well ask: are men still called to give up their lives in the service of Jesus and therefore in the service of others? Are they really supposed to lay down their lives for others?

How does the modern man 'man up'?

First, let me clarify that the Bible understands 'persons' as individuals, but not in isolation. We are best understood in relationship—in relation to God, and in relation to one another. That means that who or what a man is, and what masculinity looks like in the Bible, is described in terms of a man's relationships with others—for example, as a son, as a brother, as a husband, as a father, as a servant or as a master, and ultimately as a creature to his Creator. It is as a man lives out these relationships that he is to demonstrate masculinity. (While some of these relationships are common to men and women, such as creature–Creator, many are specific to males, such as husband and father.)

We'll think in much more depth about some of these relationships in later chapters. But for now, let's have a brief look at some specific sections of the Bible to identify the positive aspects of masculinity and remove the temptation for it to be used negatively. As you read the list below, look for the expectation or assumption that men have power in relationships—for example, as son, father or husband. (By 'power', I mean the ability to affect other people; sometimes this might be called 'authority', 'strength' or 'influence'. I've used 'power' as an overall term to bring these together.) It is true that men have power in one-to-one relationships, in family relationships, and often in wider circles as well. We'll think about each of these relationships in more detail in the second half of the book, but for now I want you take a quick but careful look at how that power is to be used in every example below.

As a son

"You have let go of the commands of God and are holding on to human traditions. ... You have a fine way of setting aside the commands of God in order to observe your own traditions! For Moses said, 'Honour your father and mother,' and, 'Anyone who curses their father or mother is to be put to death.' But you say that if anyone declares that what might have been used to help their father or mother is Corban (that is, devoted to God)—then you no longer let them do anything for their father or mother. Thus you nullify the word of God by your tradition that you have handed down. And you do many things like that." (Mark 7:8-13)

Jesus is speaking to the religious leaders of his day, and he is angry. He is angry that they are deliberately avoiding the fifth commandment ("Honour your father and your mother", from Exodus 20:12). His point is that the commandment involves an obligation to use your resources to provide for and care for your parents. The religious leaders of Jesus' day were playing 'bush lawyers' on technicalities to avoid this obligation.

As a husband

Husbands, love your wives and do not be harsh with them. (Col 3:19)

Husbands, love your wives, just as Christ loved the church and gave himself up for her ... In this same way, husbands ought to love their wives as their own bodies. He who loves his wife loves himself. (Eph 5:25, 28)

Husbands, in the same way be considerate as you live with your wives, and treat them with respect as the weaker partner and as heirs with you of the gracious gift of life, so that nothing will hinder your prayers. (1 Pet 3:7)

Husbands have power in their marriages, not simply because they are usually bigger and stronger than their wives, but because in a Christian marriage wives are told by God to be submissive to their husbands. This potentially puts women at a disadvantage and makes them vulnerable unless the man sees his God-commanded obligations clearly (and we should see them very clearly). A husband's power is to be used to take the initiative to love and serve and care for his wife—in fact, to lay down his life for her day by day.

IMPORTANT NOTE
A husband is never told to make his wife submit. Never! Men need to get this clear. She's called on to make a willing response to her husband's loving and sacrificial care for her. But it's her decision to do this before God.

As a father

Fathers, do not exasperate your children; instead, bring them up in the training and instruction of the Lord. (Eph 6:4)

Fathers, do not embitter your children, or they will become discouraged. (Col 3:21)

Fathers have power. It's obvious when kids are little, because you control pretty much everything they do. This power dynamic will change over a couple of decades, but while fathers have it, they are to use this power to instruct, nurture and train their children as they grow.

As a master

> And masters,[6] treat your slaves in the same way. Do not threaten them, since you know that he who is both their Master and yours is in heaven, and there is no favouritism with him. (Eph 6:9)

You're getting the idea by now. Masters—especially in the ancient world—have power, but how is it to be used? Fairly. They must treat those under them as they would like to be treated by God, who is master of all. In the letter to Philemon preserved in the New Testament, the apostle Paul calls on Philemon (a master) to be courageous and generous and to treat Onesimus, a returning runaway slave, in a totally countercultural way: as a brother (Phlm 15-16).

As a church leader or pastor

> Do not rebuke an older man harshly, but exhort him as if he were your father. Treat younger men as brothers, older women as mothers, and younger women as sisters, with absolute purity. (1 Tim 5:1-2)

Paul tells Timothy to be careful in how he relates to others as a church leader. He is not to be harsh with older men, and he must treat those younger than him as peers. Also, he must be especially careful in how he relates to older and younger women.

---

6   While the feminine version of the word *kurios* ('master') is used in 2 John 1 and 5, Ephesians 6:9 uses the masculine form of the word, suggesting that this command is particularly directed towards male 'masters'.

As a younger man

I write to you, young men, because you are strong, and the word of God lives in you, and you have overcome the evil one. (1 John 2:14)

In the same way, you who are younger, submit yourselves to your elders. All of you, clothe yourselves with humility toward one another, because,

"God opposes the proud
but shows favour to the humble." (1 Pet 5:5)

Similarly, encourage the young men to be self-controlled. (Titus 2:6)

You who are young, be happy while you are young,
and let your heart give you joy in the days of your youth.
Follow the ways of your heart
and whatever your eyes see,
but know that for all these things
God will bring you into judgement. (Eccl 11:9)

With young men, note the assumed strength and energy, but also the need to learn humility, to learn from your elders, to learn to be self-controlled (to control strength and hormones and impulses). Strength, energy, vitality and passion are all good things in the biblical worldview, in fact so good they need to be controlled so they aren't wasted or used in the wrong way.

As an older man

Teach the older men to be temperate, worthy of respect, self-controlled, and sound in faith, in love and in endurance. (Titus 2:2)

Those who are "older men", sometimes also translated as "elders", are to be worthy of respect and self-controlled. That is, they are to demonstrate the character and actions that are a model to younger men. Older men carry the responsibility of setting an example for others. The way they live will influence the younger generation (cf. 1 Pet 5:1-3).

As a man (more generally)

> Therefore I want the men everywhere to pray, lifting up holy hands without anger or disputing. (1 Tim 2:8)

Men are expected to pray, and not to fall into the temptation of anger or pushing their weight around in either verbal or physical conflict.

> Be alert, stand firm in the faith, act like a man, be strong. Your every action must be done with love. (1 Cor 16:13-14, HCSB)[7]

Interestingly, the apostle Paul uses the Greek word *andrizomai*—which literally means "to act like a man". In context, he's urging the Corinthians to put into practice everything he's told them in his letter. To "act like a man" involves standing firm, being strong, and acting in love. Paul is calling both men and women to show courage, but this characteristic is described as having a particularly masculine flavour.

Biblical masculinity lived out

When a man lives with healthy, biblical masculinity, he will make those around him feel safe. I saw this very clearly a few years ago when my good friend Tony was leaving as administrator of the

---

7   There are several very good English translations of the Bible (which was originally written in Hebrew, Aramaic and Greek). In most cases, I've used the New International Version (NIV). In a few cases, I've used other versions—either the Holman Christian Standard Bible (HCSB) or the King James Version (KJV)—because, for those particular verses, the translation is slightly clearer.

church where we both worked. As Tony was leaving, the other administrative staff (mainly younger women) were feeling anxious about his departure. They were wondering how they would cope without him. At Tony's farewell, Phillip, our senior pastor, said something very insightful to the other office staff: "I understand that you feel anxious about Tony leaving, and in some ways that's a good thing, because it shows he is a man who makes the people around him feel safe". What a great compliment to a man: strong and competent, he brings a feeling of safety and security to the people around him. That is healthy, biblical masculinity.

In the earlier sections of this book, we've seen that masculinity is often mocked, derided as toxic or as power that must be diluted—indeed, glossed over with nail polish. But the Bible brings a positive alternative vision of masculinity: the responsibility to nurture, protect and provide. And we have developed a nuanced understanding that, while gender is binary, masculinity and femininity need to be understood in concert with one another (e.g. Gen 2:18-25).

The message of the New Testament is that being a man is good (and being a woman is good, too); that acting as a man is good, and that men should not be embarrassed or apologetic about the power they have in relationships. (As I said above, by 'power' I mean the ability to affect other people.) This power may arise simply because of the structure of relationships, because of physical traits, or because of hierarchies that inevitably form. We shouldn't be embarrassed, dismissive, naïve or unaware about this power we have. We should embrace it, but we must be very careful how we use it, knowing that God will hold us accountable. After all, power shows what a person's heart is like. Power is the opportunity to serve, protect, provide, nurture, train, encourage, protect the truth, invest in the future, and above all to love and care for those around us.

Flowing out of all that, I'd like to propose a definition or description of healthy masculinity:

> **Healthy masculinity** is a willingness to take responsibility and use the power you have to care for and nurture those around you.

Women's magazine editor and author Phil Barker has much to say on men and masculinity. There's much I disagree with him on, but we agree completely on this point: "Men should hold it as a privilege to protect and provide with their strength. Our physical power enables us to care for those we love. But with that comes the responsibility to resist the corruptible influence of power."[8] To live this way is costly; by definition, it will be sacrificial. In the New Testament, leadership always involves the sacrificial service of others. Jesus himself taught that the way to greatness in God's eyes is to serve others (Mark 10:35-45).

I'm not expecting to change the world with this book, but I do hope to influence you to make a difference in the part of the world that you care about most—with the people around you, the ones you live with and are near each day. As a man, you have great power. You possess the power to love, care, protect, teach, encourage, serve, train and rebuke. It's there, but it costs to live this way. It means being a grown-up, showing self-discipline, leaving behind the selfish boy in all of us. It's actually what Jesus calls people to do when they follow him: to say 'no' to self, and to live a life of service—to pursue greatness in the eyes of God. Remember what Jesus said about following him:

---

8   P Barker, *The Revolution of Man: Rethinking what it means to be a man*, Allen & Unwin, 2019, p 225.

"Whoever wants to be my disciple must deny themselves and take up their cross and follow me. For whoever wants to save their life will lose it, but whoever loses their life for me and for the gospel will save it." (Mark 8:34-35)

The call to follow Jesus is a call to put him and the needs of others ahead of ourselves and our own needs, and to say no to our own selfish agenda. It seems counterintuitive—until you try it. Jesus promises that in doing this, we'll actually find life; we'll save our lives. If we ignore him and live for ourselves, we'll ultimately lose our lives.

Let me put this another way: what makes our lives worth living is not how much money we have or how 'successful' we are, but relationships. It's about what we share with other people: love, commitment and friendship. Selfishness ultimately ruins relationships. "Me and myself first" means life begins to shrink down. Relationships shrivel because of selfishness. And we won't just be short-changing our relationships in the here-and-now; to say no to a relationship with God (the one who gives life itself) will mean that we will lose our life eternally.

I've said that to be a man or to have healthy masculinity is about a willingness to take responsibility and to care for people. Different men have different challenges put before them. I've heard John Anderson, the former Deputy Prime Minister of Australia (1999-2005), tell the story of what happened on September 11, 2001 when he was Acting Prime Minister. Mr Anderson had finally managed a few hours of sleep after working nonstop for days on the financial meltdown of Ansett, one of Australia's largest airlines. He'd been trying to find a solution that would keep Ansett in the air and get passengers home. But in the early hours of the morning of September 12 (Australian time), he was awoken by a phone call and told to turn on the TV. The planes had just flown into the Twin Towers. John Howard, then Prime

Minister, was in Washington and was uncontactable. Everything was in total confusion, and John Anderson was in the hot seat. Under immense pressure, he rose to the challenge of being the calming presence that the whole country needed.

There's another man I deeply respect—a man who acted on a very different scale, but with a similar heart. At age 54, in November 2005, Peter Boyce moved to Afghanistan to work with the International Assistance Mission. Peter had lived in Sydney for most of his life, and is a vintage car nut. He's mad about giant old Packards. He maintains them, rebuilds them, and drives them as something special for the occasional wedding. The International Assistance Mission had invited him to work with them—if you can build and maintain vintage cars in Australia, you can keep vehicles going anywhere, even in Afghanistan. Around Easter 2006, after a six-month language course, Peter was just settling into his new life when, during a phone call to his mother in Australia, he realized she was unable to care for herself. She had developed Alzheimer's Disease, and wasn't cooking or eating properly. She needed a full-time carer, and there was no-one else to do the job. So Peter packed up, left his job in Afghanistan, and went to care for his mother.

It may not seem like a big sacrifice, and it's not nearly as dramatic as leading an entire nation through the trauma of 9/11. At the time, Peter's mother lived at Sapphire Beach near Coffs Harbour, which is a very pretty place. Yet it was a significant sacrifice: he gave four-and-a-half years of his life to care for her full-time, until she died. He still says, "It was a privilege to be able to see her continue to live in the place that she loved to the end of her life". Peter is now back in Sydney, working and spending time managing a men's shed in the inner city so he can care for blokes and speak about knowing Jesus to those who have open ears.

The acting prime minister, and the single man caring for his dying mother—both men who follow Jesus, and both men willingly taking responsibility, using their power to care for and nurture those around them.

I'm still working on living this way, and I've got a long way to go. But I do know that with each small step along the way, as I've followed Jesus, life has opened up more and more. It's not easy, but it is the way we find life.

So here's the challenge. You have the ability to make a difference in the lives of those around you. I've called it 'power', but you can use other labels if you like. Whatever you want to call that ability, what are you doing with it to care for and make life better for the people around you? We'll all have different roles in life— maybe as a son, husband, father, friend, colleague, or maybe even in our interactions with strangers. Wherever you find yourself, don't underestimate the power you have in those relationships— power to affect lives for good.

It's possible to go through life on the back foot, feeling like we're powerless to make a difference. I assure you, you are not powerless, and you can make a difference. The difference in someone else's life may be small, but it will be real. Start looking for those opportunities, and you'll be surprised how many there are and how much difference you can make. But it means leaving self behind; it means deliberately choosing to serve others, and that is not an easy lesson to learn.

What does it look like on a day-to-day level? That's what this book is about: how to man up in the way that we live in relationship with others. But before we get on to those roles and opportunities, let's look at the transition from being a boy to being a man—and the lessons all boys need to learn.

4. INITIATION: FROM BOYS TO MEN

ARE YOU A MAN or a boy? The answer to that question is not about age, nor is it about whether you need to shave. You can be a 50-year-old boy, or an 18-year-old man (I've met both). It's all about how you relate to other people. Steve Biddulph nailed it when, during a radio interview, he said, "Boys care about themselves; men care for other people".

In this chapter, I want to look at what a boy needs to learn in order to become a man. Are there key lessons he needs to take on board, or experiences he needs to have, before he can truly take his place as a man? And why are these necessary?

A number of books on manhood argue for reinstituting some kind of 'initiation ceremony' to facilitate the passage from boyhood to manhood. I'm not arguing that we should reintroduce these ceremonies as such, though it will do us good to look at the wisdom behind these practices, which we'll do in this chapter. But for all the changes, what has not been lost is the essential component for teaching boys how to behave and how to grow up: *other men.*

Richard Rohr's book *Adam's Return: The five promises of male initiation* is, not surprisingly, about the need for some kind of male initiation. Historically, the transition from boys to men has consistently involved the key element of older men teaching younger men 'how to be men', so that they can take their place as useful and productive members of society. Rohr points out that all traditional cultures did this, but that the modern Western world has lost this tradition:

> We are not a healthy culture for boys or men. Not the only reason, but surely one reason is that we are no longer a culture of elders who know how to pass on wisdom, identity, and boundaries to the next generation. Most men are over-mothered and under-fathered.[1]

In *Manhood in the Making*, David Gilmore talks about the male initiation rituals of many cultures around the world. One that stands out is what happens among the Maasai of East Africa. He tells the story of Tepilit Ole Saitoti, a boy who confronted and killed a huge lioness that had killed some of his family's cattle and threatened the children. This seemed to qualify him in his father's eyes to approach manhood. Gilmore quotes Tepilit: "Two months after I had killed the lioness, my father summoned all of us together. In the presence of all his children he said, 'We are going to initiate Tepilit into manhood'." Part of the initiation involved being circumcised. Tepilit was warned, "Don't move a muscle or even blink [during the ceremony]. ... The slightest movement on your part will mean you are a coward, incompetent and unworthy to be a Masai [*sic*] man."[2] Okay, the Maasai are hard men. Killing a lion only gets you on the waiting list to become a man. And as for the circumcision story—well, I flinch just pulling out nose hair.

Obviously I'm not advocating for this kind of initiation, but Richard Rohr's point is still relevant. Our culture has lost some-

---

1   R Rohr, *Adam's Return: The five promises of male initiation*, Crossroad, 2004, pp 12-13.
2   TO Saitoti, *The Worlds of a Maasai Warrior: An autobiography*, University of California Press, 1986, pp 65-66, quoted in Gilmore, *Manhood in the Making*, p 142.

thing in no longer intentionally teaching our boys what it means to be men. Initiations in traditional cultures were designed to teach young men the hard truths they needed to learn so they could be useful members of society—productive husbands, fathers and elders of the culture. One of the side effects of having lost this initiation process in the Western world is the extended adolescence of young men. Rohr points out what's becoming more obvious in Western culture: there are a growing number of boys who are not engaged in the real world and who live in a virtual world of video games or pornography.

So, without lions to kill and without the steely resolve necessary for un-anaesthetized circumcision, what do we need to learn and why is it so important? Richard Rohr presents five hard truths that, traditionally, a boy had to learn in his initiation into manhood. Rohr explains: "These are five essential messages that a man [had] to know experientially if he [was] to be rightly aligned with reality. ... The initiation correctly aligned the man so that he would not just survive in reality but thrive."[3] Why is it important to align with reality? Well, you can operate out of sync with reality if you want to, but it will only work for so long. It's like jumping off a tall building: things are still fine, but for a limited time; at some point deceleration trauma is going to kick in. Eventually, reality bites.

These five hard truths are about wisdom and about growing up so you can become a useful adult. What is interesting, though not surprising, is that all of these truths are clearly taught in the Bible. The Bible has real wisdom for life and will tell us how to align ourselves with the reality that the Creator God has made. As you read through the list, think about how many of these truths you have embraced for yourself. If you're a dad with a young son, you may want to look hard at these truths. If you

3   Rohr, *Adam's Return*, p 32.

agree with them, how are you going to work at teaching them to your boy? If not a son, is there another boy in your life you can encourage this way? This is wisdom he will need to face life.

Let's have a look at these five truths as identified by Richard Rohr. We'll consider the hard side first, then turn to consider the good news that the Bible gives. This will help us to embrace these truths rather than bury our heads in the sand.[4] This may not be an initiation exactly, but these are five truths the Bible says all men need to learn.

The first hard truth: Life is hard

When Jordan Peterson travelled around the Western world and spoke in auditoriums filled mainly with millennials, he told them essentially that *life is a catastrophe filled with inevitable suffering, and you need to be ready for it, so get your act together.* Was there ever a more prescient message right before the arrival of COVID-19?

Peterson was speaking the truth. Life *is* hard. It's strange that this seems like a new idea to so many. There is a great temptation in the Western world today to deny this, or at least to have the expectation that life will always be comfortable and involve the fulfilment of all our dreams. After all, "I'm special, I'm unique, and I can do anything I set my heart on". This nonsense begins with the phenomenon of 'helicopter parenting', a term used to describe parents who hover over their offspring, watching their every move, intervening the second anything goes wrong. 'Snowplow parenting' is the latest label to arrive on the scene, used to describe those who push every obstacle out of the way so there's nothing difficult in their child's life. Universities offer

4 Of course, these truths will also apply to women, but I'm interested here in how they will apply to boys becoming men.

'safe spaces' and insist on 'trigger warnings' so that fragile students don't encounter any turbulence in their thinking.[5]

In *The Coddling of the American Mind*, Jonathan Haidt and Greg Lukianoff show how the fragility of so many American campus students can be traced back to overprotective parenting.[6] The attempt to shield kids from everything in life that is difficult does not prepare kids for the reality of life, which can be a very tough teacher. As the old proverb goes, "Prepare a child for the road, not the road for the child". The road of life has a lot of potholes.

As we grow older, the simple wear and tear of living teaches us that life is hard. If you're younger, and especially a lot younger, then sadly those hard lessons are inevitably on their way. In fact, the trucks carrying them may have already left the depot. I guarantee, in your life you will have heartache of one kind or another. In my wider family, we have a loved one with muscular atrophy. My mum died of Alzheimer's Disease three years ago. Other families will have mothers, fathers, brothers and children who are struggling with cancer or anorexia or addictions. There are suicide attempts and self-harm, depression, and a myriad of other mental health issues. There are bosses who are bullies or colleagues who are lazy. There is retrenchment and unemployment. As I write in the middle of ongoing COVID restrictions, it seems perhaps a little unnecessary to have to convince you that there's pain in our world. Not only will your dreams almost

---

5   S Basford, 'Safe space? How an Aussie university is trying to protect students with trigger warnings', *Student Edge*, 4 April 2017, accessed 7 January 2022 (studentedge.org/article/pulling-the-trigger-how-a-university-is-trying-to-protect-students-with-trigger-warnings); J Slater, 'No place for safe spaces in Australian universities', *The Sydney Morning Herald*, 29 February 2016, accessed 7 January 2022 (smh.com.au/opinion/no-place-for-safe-spaces-in-australian-universities-20160229-gn66sl.html).

6   G Lukianoff and J Haidt, *The Coddling of the American Mind: How good intentions and bad ideas are setting up a generation for failure*, Allen Lane, 2018, pp 163-180.

certainly die the death of a thousand cuts, but you will age and feel your body inevitably begin to slow down and decay. You'll lose the people you love.

Life wasn't meant to be easy. It's a cliché, and so often an understatement. And yet this is exactly what Genesis 3 tells us to expect as a consequence of humanity walking away from the Lord. God said to Adam:

> "Because you listened to your wife and ate fruit from the tree about which I commanded you, 'You must not eat from it,'
>
>> "Cursed is the ground because of you;
>>> through painful toil you will eat food from it
>>> all the days of your life.
>> It will produce thorns and thistles for you,
>>> and you will eat the plants of the field.
>> By the sweat of your brow
>>> you will eat your food
>> until you return to the ground,
>>> since from it you were taken;
>> for dust you are
>>> and to dust you will return." (Gen 3:17-19)

Many of us will feel that something is not right as we encounter the sufferings, injustice and pain of our world. The Bible's response is *yes, that's true—something is wrong.* It is as if creation groans, which is exactly what the New Testament letter to the Romans tells us: "We know that the whole creation has been groaning as in the pains of childbirth right up to the present time" (Rom 8:22).

The Bible says God has put this pain or groaning into our world to tell us that all is not right. The pain in our world is like the pain of a broken leg—something is desperately wrong; we have walked away from God, the source of life, and the wheels are constantly falling off. In his book *The Problem of Pain*, CS Lewis puts it this way: "God whispers to us in our pleasures, speaks in our conscience, but shouts in our pain: it is His megaphone to rouse a deaf world".[7] If you aren't prepared for painful events, when they arrive (and they will) they will flatten you.

The second hard truth: You are not that important

I hope your mum thinks you're wonderful and the centre of the world. That's her job—she's your mum. The problem comes when we believe it about ourselves. Our culture's obsession with getting the perfect selfie shows just how obsessed we are with our own importance. Richard Rohr notes:

> Western comfortable people everywhere have a strong sense of deserved entitlement, and we are creating unsolvable problems for young people by enabling such a sense of entitlement, usually in the form of cheap but effusive affirmation. 'I am special' buttons and 'we are number one' banners, pinned on young people who have done little or nothing for themselves or society only trivialize the human project.[8]

It's interesting that the Bible writers regard *pride*—the belief that it's all about me (rather than God) being at the centre of the world—as the great sin. In fact, it was the original sin of the devil. The apostle Paul warns Timothy not to appoint leaders too early lest they fall into the sin of pride: any leader must be "not a novice, lest being lifted up with pride he fall into the condemnation of the devil" (1 Tim 3:6, KJV). As the Proverbs say, "when pride comes, then comes disgrace, but with humility comes wisdom" (Prov 11:2). At an even deeper level, the Genesis 3 account

---

7   CS Lewis, *The Problem of Pain*, HarperOne, 2001 [1940], p 91.
8   Rohr, *Adam's Return*, p 58.

of how every relationship—in fact all of creation—is damaged by sin centres on humanity's desire to be "like God", to be the centre of attention, to be the one who decides good and evil.[9] At its heart pride says, "It's all about me", and that self-centred heart beats in every human being.

Part of growing up, of becoming a man (or a woman), is accepting that seemingly counterintuitive truth: "I'm not the most important person in the world". If you were hit by a bus tomorrow, a few people would no doubt be shattered, a few more would be really sorry, and some would just be sorry. And then the world would move on. If we don't understand the simple truth that each of us is not *that* important, not only will we be hard to live with, but reality will have some very hard lessons in store for us.

The third hard truth: Your life is not about you

This really is counterintuitive. Of *course* my life is about me and realizing my dreams and my potential. That's the purpose of life, isn't it? It's certainly what much of our culture tells us. In her book *You Do You*, Sarah Knight counsels: "you do you" and "only you can do that".[10] The advertising blurb for the book boasts that it contains "more straight talk about how to stand up for who you are and what you really want, need, and deserve—showing when it's okay to be selfish, why it's pointless to be perfect, and how to be 'difficult'".[11] And surprise, surprise, *You Do You* was a *New York Times* bestseller—although I don't think I'd be queuing up to live with Sarah Knight.

9   "For God knows that when you eat from it your eyes will be opened, and you will be like God, knowing good and evil" (Gen 3:5).
10 S Knight, *You Do You: How to be who you are and use what you've got to get what you want*, Quercus, 2017.
11 Little, Brown and Company, *You Do You*, Little Brown website, accessed 7 January 2022 (littlebrown.com/titles/sarah-knight/you-do-you/978147899995).

The value of the 'individual' in the Western world, which ironically grew from the revolutionary teaching of Jesus and his apostles (particularly an individual's personal responsibility for how he or she relates to God directly),[12] has mutated into rampant 'individualism'. *It's all about me! I'm unique and wonderful. I must follow my dreams.*

Is it any wonder that loneliness and anxiety are on the increase?

The more we look out for number one, the more isolated we become. The more life becomes all about me and my dreams being fulfilled, the more we suffer from FOMO, sitting on the edge of commitment because we're wondering if something or someone better might come along. We can so easily start to think the world is all about us. It's forgetting this hard truth that sees us as a society grow materially richer year by year, yet with increasing levels of loneliness, isolation and anxiety.

It's possible to live a totally selfish life and prosper—for a time. It's a little like jumping off a tall building: things go quite well—for a time. In Psalm 73 in the Old Testament, Asaph complains that the proud and self-centred appear to get away with living that way. But then he sees the long view; he remembers the judgement of God on the proud who ignore him. I've already said reality is a tough teacher; it may not be in a hurry, but the lessons will arrive eventually. The more selfish someone is, and the more they live just for self, the more their life will shrink down until eventually they end up alone.

Part of becoming a man rather than a boy is being able to see that long view—that our lives have purpose in the service of others, starting with our Creator. It may seem counterintuitive at first, but Jesus says it's in taking the long view, in giving up our

12 L Siedentop, *Inventing the Individual: The origins of Western liberalism*, Allen Lane, 2014.

lives for him, that we'll find life. We've already seen in Mark's Gospel that Jesus says:

> "Whoever wants to be my disciple must deny themselves and take up their cross and follow me. For whoever wants to save their life will lose it, but whoever loses their life for me and for the gospel will save it." (Mark 8:34-35)

In some ways that's the theme of this whole book: showing that healthy masculinity—being a man—is about living in the service of others.

The fourth hard truth: You are not in control

How much of our lives do we really control? As you look back at your life, there will be many key moments, decisions you made, people you met, and events that happened that in hindsight affected the whole direction of your life. At the time, you probably had no idea they were so significant. The Old Testament book of Ecclesiastes asks hard questions about what life looks like if we live simply "under the sun" (i.e. if God is absent and "the sun" is all there is above us). At that superficial level, life seems completely random:

> I have seen something else under the sun:
>
> > The race is not to the swift
> >   or the battle to the strong,
> > nor does food come to the wise
> >   or wealth to the brilliant
> >   or favour to the learned;
> > but time and chance happen to them all. (Eccl 9:11)

These uncontrolled events can be good or bad. For example, take these two stories about men with similar names but very different story endings.

If you live in Australia, you've probably heard the story of Steven Bradbury. Bradbury won the gold medal in the 1,000 m short track skating at the 2002 Winter Olympics. He was in last place, way off the pace with seemingly no chance to win, until all his opponents were involved in a huge pile-up on the very last corner. His medal was a big deal in Australia because he was the first athlete from the Southern Hemisphere to win a Winter Olympic gold medal.

I'm not taking anything away from him—it was ten years of hard work just to be a starter in that race—but it was the uncontrollable nature of 'chance' that gave him the medal and changed his life forever.

Our second example is a sad one. Management guru Stephen Covey wrote the bestseller *The 7 Habits of Highly Successful People* and many other books about how to take control of your life. His books are useful (I'm still trying to learn some of those habits), and it could be said that if anyone had life under control, it was Stephen Covey. But in April 2012, Mr Covey was involved in a random bicycle accident in Utah and died weeks later in hospital. Control of our life is at best partial, and in reality an illusion.

It's interesting to stop and think about how few things in life we can control. I don't just mean we can't control the weather, housing market, stock market, national politics, random accidents, illnesses and disease. What about the fact that we can't control every other person on the planet, or even the people we care about most in the world? We can't control them—and if you try, you'll mess things up. The only person on the planet that we are responsible for controlling is ourselves, and that's hard enough.

Learning we're not in control is a vitally important lesson, as the New Testament book of James confirms:

> Now listen, you who say, "Today or tomorrow we will go to this or that city, spend a year there, carry on business and

make money." Why, you do not even know what will happen tomorrow. What is your life? You are a mist that appears for a little while and then vanishes. (Jas 4:13-14)

As James (the half-brother of Jesus and a leader of the early Christian church) writes these words, he's reaching back centuries earlier to the wisdom found in the Old Testament book of Proverbs: "Do not boast about tomorrow, for you do not know what a day may bring" (Prov 27:1). James and Proverbs were written centuries ago, and yet speak very directly to our lives now. We have had a very clear lesson in this, both as individuals and as a society, with the chaos caused by COVID-19. Are we going to learn the lesson?

The fifth hard truth: You are going to die

Given that the mortality rate hovers around 100 percent, it is strange that we rarely speak about death. We live in a society built on hedonism, and the hedonist worships youth and sex and fears old age and death. And so we move the old and the dying into institutions, keeping them safely out of sight. Woody Allen famously stated, "I don't want to achieve immortality through my work; I want to achieve immortality through not dying. I don't want to live in the hearts of my countrymen; I want to live in my apartment." I obviously wouldn't endorse a lot of what Woody Allen has done, but he's right about our reluctance to face up to death. Yet that's exactly what we need to do: face up to the fact that we will die. There's nothing more certain.

Ecclesiastes says, "It is better to go to a house of mourning than to go to a house of feasting, for death is the destiny of everyone; the living should take this to heart" (Eccl 7:2). This is quite literally saying that it's better for us to go to a funeral than to go to a party. (This is my standard funeral talk; I don't relish giving it, but it definitely cuts through in a chapel full of people staring at a coffin.) Ecclesiastes is not saying it's *more fun* to go to a funeral, or that we should *look forward* to funerals, but that a funeral is where we will learn wisdom—wisdom we won't get at a party.

Think on it. Embrace it.

You will die.

What will you do with that fact?

———

So, there you have it. Five hard but important truths:

- Life is hard.
- You are not that important.
- Your life is not about you.
- You are not in control.
- You are going to die.

Why do they matter? Because they will align us with reality. It's accepting these five hard truths, understanding them, even embracing them, that will allow us to make the transition from boyhood to manhood. They will change the way we treat other people and will reframe what really matters in our lives.

I know this can seem harsh or grim, but it's certainly not all bad news. Jesus teaches these five hard lessons, but he also makes great promises to those who will trust him—promises that give a great upside to each of these truths. Understanding them in light of God's wisdom is what truly sets us free. Let's walk through them.

Answer 1: Life is hard, but ...

Being a follower of Jesus doesn't make you immune from suffering. But it does help you to see hard times in a different light. The book of Romans promises that, for the man who follows or trusts

Jesus as his Lord, everything will work together for his good. That "good" is to be moulded day by day to be more like Jesus:

> And we know that in all things God works for the good of those who love him, who have been called according to his purpose. For those God foreknew he also predestined to be conformed to the image of his Son, that he might be the firstborn among many brothers and sisters. (Rom 8:28-29)

The easy times don't change us much; it's the hard things that teach us lessons. This understanding will change how we see the hard things in life, and will make us rethink what we want for the ones we love, especially our children.

John Roberts, Chief Justice of the United States Supreme Court, gave an address at his son's middle school graduation in June 2017.[13] Here is an excerpt from his speech:

> From time to time in the years to come, I hope you will be treated unfairly, so that you will come to know the value of justice. I hope that you will suffer betrayal because that will teach you the importance of loyalty. Sorry to say, but I hope you will be lonely from time to time so that you don't take friends for granted. I wish you bad luck, again, from time to time so that you will be conscious of the role of chance in life and understand that your success is not completely deserved and that the failure of others is not completely deserved either. And when you lose, as you will from time to time, I hope every now and then your opponent will gloat over your failure. It is a way for you to understand the importance of sportsmanship. I hope you'll be ignored so you know the importance of listening to others, and I hope

---

13 Roberts is described as a devoted Catholic; see J Turley, 'The faith of John Roberts', *Los Angeles Times*, 25 July 2005, accessed 7 January 2022 (latimes.com/archives/la-xpm-2005-jul-25-oe-turley25-story.html).

you will have just enough pain to learn compassion. Whether I wish these things or not, they are going to happen. And whether you benefit from them or not will depend on your ability to see the message in your misfortunes.[14]

He's right. Life will be hard. What matters is how we respond. The man who follows Jesus can know that God will use hard things, hard times, to mould and change him. It doesn't mean those difficulties won't be painful, but it does mean the Christian man faces them in a different way.

Answer 2: You are not that important, but …

It's worth considering what gives an item its value. Value is often determined by what someone is willing to pay for that item. Australia's greatest ever cricketer, the legendary Don Bradman, wore a standard Australian 'baggy green cap' during his final Ashes Tour of England in 1948. In 2017, that cap sold for over $400,000.[15] It's just a cap, but obviously it's of great value to one particular cricket tragic.

As men, we are made in the image of God. He created us, and he owns us. One of the key themes in the Bible is redemption. That means essentially paying a price to buy someone back. It's the act of saving someone from a penalty or slavery, a very similar idea to 'ransom'. In his generosity, God chose to "redeem" us or buy us back from the deserved penalty for walking away from him, breaking his laws and ignoring him as the source of life. The price of that redemption was Jesus' death in our place. The Bible says we are not our own, for we were bought at a price—the

14 Quoted in Lukianoff and Haidt, *The Coddling of the American Mind*, p 198.
15 AG Staff, 'Don Bradman's baggy green to be auctioned off for $150,000', *Australian Geographic*, 27 July 2017, accessed 7 January 2022 (australiangeographic.com.au/news/2017/07/don-bradmans-baggy-green-to-be-auctioned-off-for-150-000).

precious blood of Christ Jesus: "For you know that it was not with perishable things such as silver or gold that you were redeemed from the empty way of life handed down to you from your ancestors, but with the precious blood of Christ, a lamb without blemish or defect" (1 Pet 1:18-19).

You are not more important than other people; nor am I. But you are made in the image of God. And if you belong to Jesus and follow him, you are loved by God—so much so that he gave his only Son so that you can become part of his family.

In other words, your value is determined by what someone was willing to pay for you.

Answer 3: Your life is not about you, but ...

As discussed in chapter 3, it's a beautiful irony that as we give our life to the service of Jesus and therefore to the service of others, our lives grow and become bigger. Part of learning God's wisdom is understanding that it's not wrong to want greatness or to want to live a great life; it's a matter of how and where we pursue that 'greatness'. Jesus tells his followers James and John the way to real greatness in the eyes of God:

> "... whoever wants to become great among you must be your servant, and whoever wants to be first must be slave of all. For even the Son of Man did not come to be served, but to serve, and to give his life as a ransom for many." (Mark 10:43-45)

Answer 4: You are not in control, but ...

In the middle of what seems like a chaotic world, we can often feel lost, like our world is out of control. But there is a hand on the wheel. We can have confidence that God has all things in his hands. As Jesus says in the Sermon on the Mount:

"Therefore I tell you, do not worry about your life, what you will eat or drink; or about your body, what you will wear. Is not life more than food, and the body more than clothes? Look at the birds of the air; they do not sow or reap or store away in barns, and yet your heavenly Father feeds them. Are you not much more valuable than they? Can any one of you by worrying add a single hour to your life?

"And why do you worry about clothes? See how the flowers of the field grow. They do not labour or spin. Yet I tell you that not even Solomon in all his splendour was dressed like one of these. If that is how God clothes the grass of the field, which is here today and tomorrow is thrown into the fire, will he not much more clothe you—you of little faith?" (Matt 6:25-30)

Notice Jesus' "how much more" argument: if God cares for birds (unnoticed by most people) and flowers (so temporary), *how much more* will he care for the people who belong to him? Understanding and holding on to this promise makes all the difference as we face a world that can feel random and chaotic.

Answer 5: You are going to die, but ...

It is totally natural to fear death. But Jesus taught that if we belong to him we need never fear death, as even that will not separate us from him. When Jesus stood at the grave of Lazarus, he promised that those who trust him will never die spiritually, but will one day be raised to eternal life. Speaking to Lazarus' sister Martha, Jesus said:

"I am the resurrection and the life. The one who believes in me will live, even though they die; and whoever lives by believing in me will never die. Do you believe this?" (John 11:25)

We all must die—that is inevitable. For Christians, however, the sting (or great fear) of death has been removed (1 Cor 15:55-59). In fact, the New Testament refers to death as 'falling asleep' (e.g. 1 Cor 15:20; 1 Thess 4:13). We will still grieve loved ones who die knowing Jesus, but there is nothing to fear. We "do not grieve like the rest of mankind, who have no hope" (1 Thess 4:13).

———

At the end of this chapter, I think a hard word may be in order to some men, especially some younger men. These words come from observation and heartache as I look around me.

The loss of these truths in our culture is not a trivial matter. It's the reason we have males in their 20s and 30s who are still just boys. It's the reason we have continued adolescence, or 'failure to launch' as it's now called. We have boys addicted to video games in the virtual world instead of making a difference in the real world. We have boys who won't commit to marrying their long-term girlfriends, or who live in future fantasies of being famous rather than growing up, taking responsibility as men, and making a difference in the world. It's a hard word, but it's important to ask ourselves: *Have I learned these hard truths about myself?*

Let's not worry about subtlety.

Have you understood that life is going to be hard?

Do you realize that you're not that important?

Do you know that your life is not about you?

Do you accept that you aren't in control?

Do you realize that, one day, you are going to die?

If you're a follower of Jesus, you are called to grow up and take responsibility. I don't think we'll ever fully arrive at living this way. I know I find it easy to drift or lose focus, partly because there are so many voices that whisper lies in our ears. I need to keep on being reminded about these hard truths. And so do you. Because "the truth will set you free" (John 8:32).[16] These truths will mean we can live with a healthy masculinity. They will reframe what really matters in our lives and will set us free to be men who make wise life choices and are able to invest in the lives of others.

Let's now move to a couple of chapters on how to live all this out, before looking at some of the specific relationships we may have as men.

---

16 See C Pope, 'Five hard truths that will set you free', *Community in Mission blog*, 11 July 2017, accessed 7 January 2022 (blog.adw.org/2017/07/five-hard-truths-will-set-free).

5. HOW TO LOOK AFTER FUTURE YOU

IN ONE OF THE FINAL episodes of the TV drama *Rake* about lawyer Cleaver Green, a man whose life is in constant chaos, his son asks him, "Dad, why are you such a screw-up?" After a moment's thought, he answers, "I guess I lack a sense of life's continuity". I'm beginning to realize how important that sense of life's continuity is for being able to enjoy life, now and in the future. You need to be able to enjoy the *now*, but also be able to look after Future You.

In fact, Present You and how well you're doing now is very much a function of how well Past You looked after Future You. As you think about your life, there may well be things that Present You would want to say to Past You about how he should have behaved.

So how do you look after Future You? There are two key ideas.

Idea 1: Self-control

It doesn't sound very exciting, and yet the irony is that self-control is the way to have real freedom. How? Let's start with a definition from the *Oxford Dictionary*: self-control is "the ability to control one's self, in particular one's emotions and desires, especially in difficult situations".

Who is in control? It's you—not hormones, not chemical substances, not other people's opinions. The 'self' is in control. But self-control is not easy.

Daniel Akst is a New York journalist who has written an entire book on just how tough it is to have self-control.[1] He claims our evolutionary past hasn't caught up with the power of today's choices:

> Humans evolved with the capacity to look ahead and guide themselves accordingly, deferring gratification when it seemed useful to do so, but we didn't evolve to cope with a world where we could obtain luscious food at a moment's notice, encounter thousands of strangers in a single afternoon, or spend next year's earnings with a few swipes of plastic. Modern life simply requires an unnatural degree of self-control, and one of its side effects is self-control fatigue.[2]

He then takes his readers on a tour of the modern world, especially the internet. He looks at gambling, sex, pornography, food, alcohol and spiralling credit card debt. He puts forward no real answers, but he does offer one excellent insight regarding the battle within: "what matters, when it comes to self-control, isn't so much willpower as vision—the ability to see the future, so that the long-run consequences of our short-run choices are vividly clear ... self-control is all about seeing beyond the moment—about deferring gratification".[3] Notice he mentions 'delayed gratification', which is our second key idea.

---

1 D Akst, *We Have Met the Enemy: Self-control in an age of excess*, Penguin Press, 2011.
2 Akst, *We Have Met the Enemy*, p 153.
3 Akst, *We Have Met the Enemy*, p 14.

THE MANUAL

Idea 2: Delayed gratification

How is this different from self-control? Self-control is the way to have freedom in your life. Delayed gratification is how you can look after Future You. Let's drill down a little more.

The *Encyclopedia Britannica* defines delayed gratification in this way: "the act of resisting an impulse to take an immediately available reward in the hope of obtaining a more valued reward in the future". Delayed gratification is the way to look after Future You, and we're not thinking right when we ignore this. As an example of 'not thinking', who better than Homer Simpson? In *The Simpsons* episode 'MoneyBart', Marge is asking Homer to help coach the kids' baseball team. He refuses. Marge says, "You know, someday these kids will be out of the house, and you'll regret not spending more time with them". Homer responds, "That's a problem for future Homer. Man, I don't envy that guy", (as he pours a bottle of vodka into a jar of mayonnaise, shakes it, and collapses after drinking the contents).[4] We can live not envying our future self, but we'll be setting ourselves up for a world of pain. Or we can understand delayed gratification.

One of the gurus of delayed gratification is Walter Mischel, the man who devised 'the Marshmallow Test'. Mischel was a Professor of Psychology at Stanford University in the 1960s, when he began a study of the long-term effects of delayed gratification by experimenting with preschoolers. With parental permission, he would sit a preschool or kindergarten child at a desk in a room on their own and put one marshmallow on a plate in front of them. They would be told they could eat that marshmallow right now, or they could wait until the adult running the experiment came back in a few minutes. If the first marshmallow was uneaten, they'd be given a second marshmallow to eat as

---

4   N Kruse (director), 'MoneyBart' [television program], *The Simpsons* (season 22, episode 3), Fox Broadcasting, 2010.

well. The footage of a similar experiment playing out as the kids wait, desperately trying not to eat the first marshmallow, is highly entertaining.[5] Mischel and his psychology students then tracked these children over several decades of their lives. The study notes:

> What the preschoolers did as they tried to keep waiting, and how they did or didn't manage to delay gratification, unexpectedly turned out to predict much about their future lives. The more seconds they waited at age four or five, the higher their college-admission SAT scores and the better their rated social and cognitive function in adolescence. At age 27-32, those who had waited longer during the Marshmallow Test in preschool had a lower body mass index and a better sense of self-worth, pursued their goals more effectively, and coped more adaptively with frustration and stress. At midlife, those who could consistently wait ("high delay"), versus those who couldn't ("low delay"), were characterized by distinctively different brain scans in areas linked to addictions and obesity.[6]

In his book, Mischel not only argues that delayed gratification is the key to a successful life; he also says his experiments show it can be learned or strengthened. This can be achieved by strategies such as trying to "mentally cool the problem" or pre-commitment to a course of action once the expected temptation arrives. He concludes that perhaps the most important aspect of being able to delay gratification is the place of motivation or a burning goal.

His conclusions are similar to Daniel Akst's insights about

5   One replication of Michel's experiment is available at Watermark Community Church, 'The Marshmallow Test' [video], *Igniter Media*, YouTube, 25 September 2009, accessed 7 January 2022 (youtube.com/watch?v=QX_oy9614HQ).
6   W Mischel, *The Marshmallow Test: Understanding self-control and how to master it*, Transworld, 2014, p 5.

vision or "seeing beyond the moment". Self-control and delayed gratification aren't optional extras in life; they are the difference between success and failure, between getting on top of things or allowing them to overwhelm us. They are the difference between being a responsible and productive man or being a bag of excuses and unrealized potential. Sitting on your butt watching TV and eating Cheezels takes no self-control, no delay of gratification, and it achieves—well, you can fill in the picture.

Of course, you already know all this. If you've ever studied for an exam when you would rather be doing something else, or practised an instrument or a sport, or saved up to buy something, you've exercised self-control and pursued delayed gratification. If we're going to be productive men, we need self-control. Future You needs Present You to be able to delay gratification and to invest in the right things now.

Self-control in the Scriptures

What does the Bible have to say about self-control and delayed gratification? The New Testament talks about this topic often, mentioning self-control around a dozen times. Jesus wants his men to have freedom, and that means self-control is essential. To be blunt, there's no freedom in living at the constant mercy of every fleeting thought that crosses your mind or in being controlled by whatever hormones are pumping through your body. The promise for the man who will follow Jesus is that God will give you his Spirit, and his Spirit will be at work in you and begin to change you. The Spirit will change your character—who you are as a person.

In his letter to the Christians in Galatia (in modern-day Turkey), the apostle Paul uses the analogy of character change being like fruit growing on a tree: "the fruit of the Spirit is love, joy, peace, forbearance, kindness, goodness, faithfulness, gentleness and self-control" (Gal 5:22-23). Self-control is last on the list, not because it's the least important, but because it's *so* important in living out all these character traits. It's hard to imagine living with love, joy, peace, forbearance, kindness, goodness, faithfulness and gentleness if you don't possess self-control. The promise is that God's Spirit will be at work in the life of men who follow Jesus to give them self-control or help them develop self-control.

But how does that happen? Earlier in the same letter, Paul writes this:

> So I say, walk by the Spirit, and you will not gratify the desires of the flesh. For the flesh desires what is contrary to the Spirit, and the Spirit what is contrary to the flesh. They are in conflict with each other, so that you are not to do whatever you want. (Gal 5:16-17)

Paul is saying that the Spirit of God will move the Christian man to walk in the way of the Spirit—that is, to live Jesus' way. At the same time, the old nature, or "the flesh" as the New Testament calls it, will want to go back to the old ways. The man who follows Jesus will be aware of this struggle within. The way to develop self-control, the way to see the fruit of the Spirit in our lives, is to listen to the Spirit of God as he leads us in that right direction.

This may at first sound a bit like Daniel Akst's bigger picture mentioned earlier, or Walter Mischel's 'burning goal'. But something far more profound is happening. The Spirit of God at work in our lives will bring a deep change—not just in our actions, but in our hearts before God. It's a change so significant that the Bible writers speak of being "born again"—of spiritually coming to life in knowing God and in wanting to honour him in how we live.

So how does this happen? The Spirit of God moves the Christian man by giving understanding of God's words and promises in the Bible. God's word is alive through his Spirit at work. Listening to his words is listening to his Spirit. The Christian man will be drawn to trust the words of God as God's Spirit is at work in him. If you're not clear on what it means to follow Jesus and to experience the spiritual transformation that he brings, I've given much more detail on the how and why of following Jesus in the conclusion to this book.

Handling temptation

With regard to looking after Future You, I've aimed for this book to be overwhelmingly positive. There are so many good things for men to start doing in order to man up and to 'get on the front foot'. But there's also a time to speak about the things we need to stop and the areas of life where we need to take control.

Each of us will struggle with different temptations. Some men struggle with gambling. For me, through no moral strength at all, gambling has never been a problem. I'm the guy who can fall asleep during the Melbourne Cup (Australia's biggest horse race). If gambling is a real struggle for you, I won't trot out a lot of clichés, but you need to get some help to deal with it.

The same applies for men who have trouble controlling food consumption and their weight, or those who battle addiction to video games, for example. I have no problems controlling gambling or calories or computer games. That doesn't take great self-discipline from me. Those things just don't grab me. But there are two temptations that have been an ongoing struggle for me, and I'll write about them here because they are a struggle for so many men. My aim is not to make you feel guilty, but to help you think about your life and how to look after Future You.

The first one is *alcohol*.

The Bible says that alcohol is a good gift of God. Psalm 104 says that God makes "wine that gladdens human hearts, oil to make their faces shine" (Psalm 104:15).

We shouldn't feel guilty about enjoying a drink, especially

given that Jesus' first miraculous 'sign' was making approximately 600 litres of the very best wine at a wedding (John 2:1-11). Alcohol is a good gift from God to be enjoyed, and God in his kindness tells us how to enjoy it. He also gives us a line that we shouldn't cross. And that line is, not surprisingly, related to self-control. Our society calls it 'getting drunk' or 'being under the influence'. The Bible is clear on this. To link back to the ideas of walking with the Spirit and self-control, the apostle Paul says that it must be the Spirit of God, not alcohol, that controls men: "Do not get drunk on wine, which leads to debauchery. Instead, be filled with the Spirit ..." (Eph 5:18). It's when we disregard the maker's instructions on this good gift that so many things get messed up.

Our society refuses to come to terms with the damage that alcohol does: violence (including domestic violence), drownings, health problems (like liver failure, obesity and so many others), and road accidents. Or it just makes men plain dumb, useless and hard to live with. If you've ever had to live with a drunk, you'll understand why a good God tells us not to cross that line.

For me personally, I love a drink, particularly Corona beer and red wine. The problem is that I love it too much. I also come from a family where many men in my wider gene pool have had problems with alcohol. I have trouble putting on the brakes. I remember being on holiday in 2006. I had a few too many reds. The last glass, of course, had a headache in it. After some serious soul searching, that day—16 July 2006—I decided to look after Future Me and the rest of my family, and I stopped drinking altogether. I've not had a drink since.[7]

Because I had trouble putting on the brakes, I've taken the step of removing the wheels from the car. Does that make me a hero? No, not at all. It's just easier to stop that way—easier and simpler

---

7   I do allow myself a tiny shot glass of wine at church communion. And yes, I only go up to take communion once each time!

than trying to manage something I have trouble controlling. Why have I done this? Because I needed to bring the 'best me' to every situation. Do I miss having a drink? Only on days ending in 'y'. But Present Me is very glad that Past Me did this for Future Me.

If you're struggling with alcohol or you find that you're crossing that line of self-control, then it would be great to get some help.[8]

The second area of great temptation for me and for so many men is *pornography.*

An older male relative took me to my first pornographic movie at the age of thirteen; it has been a temptation for me ever since. But it has all changed dramatically in the past 40 or 50 years. When I was a kid, to see pornography required somehow getting hold of a pornographic magazine that would be secretly passed around the woodwork rooms at school—teenage boys with sweaty hands looking at crumpled pictures. Or it was necessary to go to one of those seedy little cinemas in low-rent areas with no windows, and sit in the dark with the raincoat-and-sandshoe brigade.

The internet has changed everything by bringing accessibility, anonymity and affordability.

Accessible? It's endless. An endless stream of visually exciting, sexually arousing images. It's in your pocket, on your desk or on any screen. It's everywhere.

Anonymous? It can be done in secret. You don't have to go anywhere. You don't need a raincoat or sandshoes. Internet browsers even have a 'private browsing' mode which leaves no record (so they tell us) of where you've been.

Affordable? It can be financially free. (Notice I didn't say totally free. Financially it might appear free, but there's always a price to pay.)

---

8   See Alcoholics Anonymous or Overcomers Outreach (overcomersoutreach.net) for help.

It's not my intention to make you feel guilty. If you're tempted by this stuff, it basically means that you're male and you have a pulse; you're in the company of a huge percentage of the male population. Pornography taps into how men are wired. Men are visually aroused, and pornography is designed specifically and powerfully to do that. This is the beast that gnaws on men's souls; it chews on our insides. It thrives on secrecy, so I need to drag it out in the sun and look at it.

Part of doing that is grasping the size and scope of the problem. Pornography is now ubiquitous. It's a massive worldwide industry. In 2018, the human race made no fewer than 33.5 billion visits to a single pornography website. That's 92 million visits every single day. This same site had 4,791,799 pornographic videos uploaded —"enough hours for a single person to continuously watch [pornography] without breaks for 115 years".[9] More generally, the level of pornography accessed through the web, and the age at which young ones are viewing it, is deeply troubling.

How does pornography work and how does it damage men? Here's a story that I think illustrates why it's so popular and so damaging at the same time.

A few years ago, I was visiting Nyngan (a small rural town in far-western New South Wales) on a feral animal reduction holiday. On one of these farms, I got talking to an old bloke at the entrance to his shed. I couldn't help but notice there were fox skins all over the wall. Foxes are a feral introduced species in Australia. In those days, fox skins were actually worth some money, as wearing fur coats hadn't become politically incorrect. The old bloke explained to me how he'd caught so many foxes. The process was simple but clever:

---

9   S Rense, 'The human race really outdid itself with porn searches in 2018', *Esquire*, 12 December 2018, accessed 13 December 2021 (esquire.com/lifestyle/sex/news/a52061/most-popular-porn-searches).

I get a dead kangaroo or something that smells pretty bad, and drag it behind the four-wheel-drive along a track in the bush. Every now and then I pull up and dip cyanide capsules in condensed milk and put them in the middle of the track where I've just dragged the bait. The fox follows the bait smell, walks along the trail, finds the condensed milk, licks it up, swallows the cyanide tablet, and bang—he's dead before he knows what's hit him.

Whether that story is completely true, I'm not sure—he may have been embellishing a little for the city boy. But my point is that that's how pornography works. We are the foxes. Pornography tastes sweet at first—sweet in the mouth. And it tastes so good as you swallow it. And yet, once swallowed, it's poison. It will kill you emotionally, relationally, sexually and spiritually. And it will be addictive even as it kills you.

It's especially poisonous for young men who haven't had much, or any, real sexual experience. But it will mess up older men as well. It gives totally unrealistic expectations about sex and what it will be like. It makes men think wrongly about the way a woman should look and behave, but it also makes men feel inadequate—with regard to 'performance', and in the wedding tackle department. I say 'performance' because that's how pornography portrays sex: it's a performance you do to someone. It removes intimacy from sex. It changes the way men think about women, too. I've known men whose entire understanding of not just sex but women in general has been poisoned by pornography.

Some men might say, "Okay, it's not ideal, but it's still basically harmless". Not so. Pornography is fiercely addictive and it messes with your brain. A lot of men I've spoken to—and I mean a *lot*—think of pornography as a kind of emotional junk food: when you're tired, flat or stressed, pornography can be like an emotional sugar hit. But it's not a sugar hit. It's bigger than that; it's a dopamine hit. Dopamine is a neurotransmitter responsible for controlling the brain's reward and pleasure centres. Because pornography activates the pleasure centres in your brain, that pleasure and arousal become addictive. Fitness blogger Bryan Ye explains it well:

> Sexual stimuli is the most dopamine inducing activity that you can naturally experience. While enjoying pornography, your dopamine levels rise to around 200% of what is normal.
>
> **These abnormal levels of dopamine [mess] with your mood.**
>
> Watching porn for extended periods of time, keeping your dopamine level so artificially high tricks our brains into thinking this is the new "normal".
>
> Since our bodies are constantly trying to achieve homeostasis, these consistently high levels of dopamine create plastic changes to the brain, desensitizing neurons so that they are less affected by it and decreasing the number of receptors available.[10]

But the problem is that, over time, you need more and newer stimuli to get the same hit. As Philip Zimbardo and Nikita Coulombe write, "Regular consumption of pornography more or less wears out your reward system. ... The sorry result is that daily life, and often sex with a familiar partner, grows duller and less rewarding."[11] There is a great irony here: as you look for excitement with pornography, it damages your brain and wears out the reward centre, which means that the rest of life grows strangely more and more grey.

There are plenty of other reasons to turn away from pornogra-

10 B Ye, *How Porn is Ruining Your Life*, Fit Yourself Club website, 2016, accessed 7 January 2022 (fityourself.club/how-porn-is-ruining-your-life-10c92d179e11).
11 Zimbardo and Coulombe, *Man Disconnected*, p 109.

phy. When I think about the way in which the whole industry literally uses and abuses young women, I'm ashamed to admit I'm tempted by the stuff. The content of pornography continues to grow more extreme and abusive: more damaging to the performers, both men and women, but particularly to the young women involved. Former pornography star Lisa Ann told *The Guardian* newspaper:

> There were times on set with people where I was like, 'This is not a good situation. This is not safe. This girl is out of her mind and we're not sure what she's going to say when she leaves here'. ... Everyone's a ticking time bomb, and a lot of it is linked to the drugs. A lot of this new pain comes from these new girls who have to do these abusive scenes, because that does break you down as a woman.[12]

We're strangely perverse creatures, really. To treat women in such a degrading way is the exact opposite of healthy masculinity, and yet so many men become addicted to this poison.[13]

The way pornography treats the actors involved is enough reason to stay away from it, but there's another more personal reason as well: it rots your own soul.

For men who follow Jesus, this is especially poisonous. The Bible verse that speaks perhaps most powerfully to this is found in 1 Peter: "Dear friends, I urge you, as foreigners and exiles, to abstain from sinful desires, which wage war against your soul" (1 Pet 2:11). Literally, Peter is speaking about "the desires of the flesh" (the old nature within us). And he says that these desires

---

12 Fight the New Drug, 'Popular porn performer Lisa Ann describes extreme abuse new performers endure', *Fight the New Drug blog*, 2 January 2019, accessed 13 December 2021 (fightthenewdrug.org/hall-of-fame-ex-porn-star-talks-extreme-damage-done-to-new-performers).

13 You can read more about the damaging effects of pornography at the website of Fight the New Drug, a non-religious organization dedicated to raising awareness of the harmful effects of pornography: fightthenewdrug.org.

wage war against our soul (or inner life). They rot us from the inside.

Like so many lies, pornography takes something good and twists it. The Bible says that sex is the gift of God, to be enjoyed within marriage (a lifelong, public commitment between one man and one woman). When sexual intimacy is enjoyed in this context, it makes a man feel strong and loved and good. Pornography is powerful, but because it cuts so strongly against God's good design for sex, it makes men feel weak and dirty and ashamed. It wars against our souls.

The great irony is that I can know all this, even research it and write it down, and still be tempted by it. So if you're tempted by it, what's the answer? It starts with seeing clearly the bigger picture of what we want. It means working hard now with a burning goal, with a vision of who we want to be. The man who follows Jesus needs to work hard at staying away from this stuff that wars against his soul. If not, it will end with those feelings of shame and weakness, and ultimately with addiction. It'll mess with our brains and cause arousal fatigue. It'll change the way we see women and even the way we see the world.

It's very hard to fight it alone. We need help. We need to fight it together. If this is a struggle for you, it's best to speak to a mature Christian man privately about it. You'll be surprised at the understanding, empathy and help you can get. To be able to talk to people and fight this together is a great help. In fact, in the world we live in, we really need other men to help us fight the temptations that will rot our souls. To live Jesus' way is a team effort; we must value and care for our brothers in the battle.

There are also effective technology solutions. I have *Covenant Eyes* on every device.[14] It does restrict some of your access to different sites, but it also sends a summarized feed of your online

14 For information about *Covenant Eyes,* visit their website: covenanteyes.com.

activity to your accountability partners—people who have agreed to help you give up looking at this stuff.

Remember, the old cliché is true: "You have two tigers within you: the good one and the bad one. The one that gets stronger is the one that you feed." What we fill our head with will determine which 'tiger' grows stronger. It really is all about seeing the big picture of what we want, or who we want to be. If you're a man who follows Jesus, he calls you to be pure in thought and action: "But among you there must not be even a hint of sexual immorality, or of any kind of impurity, or of greed, because these are improper for God's holy people" (Eph 5:3).

The great news is that Jesus also promises forgiveness and a fresh start in this area, as shown by these wonderful words that Paul wrote to the first-century church in Corinth:

> Or do you not know that wrongdoers will not inherit the kingdom of God? Do not be deceived: Neither the sexually immoral nor idolaters nor adulterers nor men who have sex with men nor thieves nor the greedy nor drunkards nor slanderers nor swindlers will inherit the kingdom of God. And that is what some of you *were*. But you were washed, you were sanctified, you were justified in the name of the Lord Jesus Christ and by the Spirit of our God. (1 Cor 6:9-11)

Some of the people in the church in Corinth had been into some bad stuff. Actually, let's call it what it is: sin. It's sin that would separate them (and us) from God permanently. But do you see the good news in the last part of those verses? They had been forgiven, changed and washed clean in the name of Jesus and by the Spirit of God. And it's the same for any man who will bring his sin to Jesus and ask for forgiveness. There is a fresh start and complete forgiveness.

And yet we must remember that with forgiveness comes repentance, turning away from this poison. We need to work hard at living a life that honours the Lord, to walk with the Spirit of God and go where he leads us.

———

I've written honestly about a couple of temptations that have been real for me, but of course there are many other issues of self-control that men struggle with (I very briefly mentioned gambling, video games and over-eating as just a few of the many examples). To be honest, I haven't dealt with these other issues because I don't really feel competent to give advice on most of them. I haven't had to 'walk a mile in these shoes', if you know what I mean.

But regardless of the specific issues you may struggle with, I can tell you this with confidence: dealing with temptation is, at its most basic level, about trust (or faith) in what Jesus says to us in his word. In the moment of decision, can I trust him? Will I trust that he knows best, and that in the long run he will care for me, so that I can delay gratification and look to him? It's about trusting that Jesus knows what's best for us now in the moment, and that he also knows what's best for Future You.

6. ENDURANCE: THE POWER OF JUST TURNING UP

"THE MASS OF MEN lead lives of quiet desperation."[1] So said American author Henry David Thoreau. He's right. There are many different reasons for this desperation. For some of us, our dreams may be dying. I don't mean the dreams we had as kids, where we realize we won't represent our country at the Olympics, but those deeply private things that we'd hoped for. Those dreams that we didn't share with anyone else. Eventually we realize these things are not going to happen.

In his book *Iron John*, Robert Bly talks about dreams turning to ashes:

> A young man in high school dreams that he will be a race driver, a mountain climber, he will marry Miss America, he'll be a millionaire by age 30, he'll get a Nobel Prize in physics by 35, he will be an architect and build the tallest building ever. He will get out of this hick town and live in Paris, he will have famous friends ... and by 35 all these dreams are ashes.[2]

The dreams that you haven't shared with anyone begin to slowly pass away, and that sense of quiet desperation lives with us. Or

1   HD Thoreau, *Walden; or, Life in the Woods*, Riverside Press, 1854, p 3.
2   R Bly, *Iron John: A book about men*, DaCapo Press, 2004, p 81.

maybe the quiet desperation comes from heartache—just the wear and tear of life. I don't know anyone who's reached middle age without major heartache of some kind, be that from a failed marriage, or wayward children, or lack of children, or wider family, or failure at work, or health issues for themselves or for someone they love. Heartache is inevitable.

Or it may just be living in 'Groundhog Day'. If you've seen the movie, you'll remember that Bill Murray plays Phil Connors, a journalist stuck in a small town in the USA, attending a strange winter ceremony about a groundhog that's supposed to predict the weather. Through some kind of time warp, he has to repeat the same day over and over again, endlessly. This endless loop begins to drive him crazy. It's easy for us to feel like we're living the same day again, and again, and again. Boredom is just a fact of life. What's really strange is that I'm able to manage to be bored and stressed at the same time, which is logically impossible but often achieved. For many men, the repetitive, mind-numbing routine of life is what they dread. Rod Dreher put it this way:

> Everydayness is my problem. It's easy to think about what you would do in wartime, or if a hurricane blows through, or if you spend a month in Paris, or if your guy wins the election, or if you won the lottery or bought that thing you really wanted. It's a lot more difficult to figure out how you're going to get through today without despair.[3]

If you scratch the surface, talking quietly with many men, the desperation is there, and it shows itself in the dumb, self-destructive things some of us do out of boredom or heartache. Some of it is the stuff we've already talked about—alcohol, or pornography, or gambling—or maybe it's the crazy toys men buy. Sometimes we'll

3 R Dreher, 'Everydayness', *The American Conservative*, 14 November 2012, accessed 7 January 2022 (theamericanconservative.com/dreher/everydayness-wallace-stevens).

latch on to anything that looks like it might distract us from that feeling of the slow "dying of the light" inside us. These dumb, self-destructive things obviously aren't the answer—but what is? What do you do with that sense of desperation? Dreams dying, or heartache, or Groundhog Day, or stress and boredom?

There are people who will tell you the answer is simply to become a Christian. If you become a follower of Jesus, they promise, then boredom or stress or disappointments will just disappear! They'll tell you that life will always feel like a wonderful adventure.

That's pretty much the message from John Eldredge in his book *Wild at Heart*, a top seller with men in its day. To his credit, Eldredge is aiming to set Christian men free from the emasculation that can come with some pale and limp versions of the Christian life. That's a fine and necessary goal. I'm all for blokes being blokes, and I'm not a fan of pale and limp. But allow me to be a little critical of the way he describes the Christian life.

Eldredge says a man needs three things: a battle to fight; a beauty to rescue; and an adventure to live. Throughout the book, he says the Christian life should be an adventure:

> "The spiritual life cannot be made suburban," said Howard Macey. "It is always frontier and we who live in it must accept and even rejoice that it remains untamed." ... So there comes a time in a man's life when he's got to break away from all that and head off into the unknown with God.[4]

Jesus calls us to follow him, and in some ways the Christian life *will* be an adventure. But it seems to me that what John Eldredge has done, with good intentions, is to baptize the American Frontier myth. I'm not convinced that's what Jesus promises. If you

---

4   J Eldredge, *Wild at Heart: Discovering the secret of a man's soul*, Thomas Nelson, 2001, pp 210, 213.

follow Jesus, yes, life will have meaning and purpose, but it will also often feel mundane.

Imagine this: it's winter, and you're going to work because you need to pay the mortgage and feed your kids. This is commute number 6,048 (only 3,952 to go). You're on the train. As you stare around the carriage, the other commuters sit or stand with the thousand-yard stare, with eyes that say, "Please kill me". And you think to yourself, "Woo-hoo, this is an adventure!"

I don't think so. It feels much more like Groundhog Day.

So what's the answer?

In the apostle Paul's letter to the Christians in Colossae (now an archaeological site in modern-day Turkey),[5] he writes about the power of God at work in their lives. This power of God shows itself in a surprising way. He writes about "being strengthened with all power according to his glorious might so that you may have great ..." (Col 1:11). The power of God and his glorious might will be at work in their lives to give them great ... what? What would you expect to read next? Great miracles? Seeing thousands become followers of Jesus? Preaching amazing sermons? Feeding crowds of thousands with a few bread rolls?

The answer is probably not what we expect: "Being strengthened with all power according to his glorious might so that you may have great *endurance* and *patience*".

It doesn't seem all that impressive at first; the power of God at work in someone's life will give them endurance and patience. Really? Is that it?

But when we pause and reflect, wisdom tells us just how powerful and impressive these character traits are. The word for 'patience' occurs in the New Testament 24 times, while the word for 'endurance' occurs 31 times. These words are often used in

---

5   You can take a tour of the ruins at Colossae for yourself (memphistours.com/ Turkey/Turkey-Travel-Guide/Antique-Cities/wiki/Colossae).

the context of continuing to trust God even when life is hard, or when it's costly to keep on living his way. But almost as often they're used in the context of just keeping on serving Jesus and caring for others—simply pressing on with doing it.[6]

The question I want us to consider here is: Do we have eyes to see that this second type of "endurance and patience", a simple commitment to 'keep on going', is the work of God's Spirit in the lives of those who follow Jesus? And how does this apply to being a man?

Remember that in chapter 4, 'From boys to men', we heard from Steve Biddulph, who said the difference between men and boys is that boys care about themselves, while men care about other people. We also heard from Jordan Peterson, who wrote:

> I tell my students: Aim to be the person at your father's funeral that everyone, in their grief and misery, can rely on. There's a worthy and noble ambition; strength in the face of adversity. That's very different from the wish for a trouble-free life.[7]

---

6   The word for 'endurance' (*hypomonē*), sometimes translated 'perseverance', is used 31 times in the New Testament. It is used 13 times in the context of enduring suffering or difficulties, i.e. continued faith and obedience in the face of hardship of various kinds (see Rom 5:3; 2 Cor 1:6, 6:4, 12:12; 2 Thess 1:4; Jas 1:3-4, 5:11; Rev 1:9, 2:3, 3:10, 13:10, 14:12). It is also used in the sense of endurance, to keep on going in obedience in the service of Jesus and other people (see Luke 8:15; Rom 8:25, 15:4-5; Col 1:11; 1 Thess 1:3; 2 Thess 3:5; 1 Tim 6:11; 2 Tim 3:10; Titus 2:2; Heb 10:36, 12:1; 2 Pet 1:6; Rev 2:2, 2:19).
   The word for 'patience' (*makrothumia*), sometimes translated 'forbearance', is used 24 times in the New Testament. Often it refers to the patience of God with people, who deserve his judgement (e.g. Rom 2:4, 9:22; 1 Tim 1:16; 2 Pet 3:9, 3:15). Eleven times, followers of Jesus are urged to be patient, e.g. in waiting for the return of Jesus (Heb 6:12; Jas 5:7-8), and in the face of suffering (Jas 5:10). Seven of these times speak of Christian character and the work of God's Spirit to bring patience in how Christian people live with others (1 Cor 13:4; 2 Cor 6:6; Gal 5:22; Eph 4:2; Col 1:11, 3:12; 1 Thess 5:14).
7   Peterson, *12 Rules for Life*, p 365.

The essence of being a man is a willingness to accept responsibility, to accept taking care of others. How do we combine that with the ordinariness of everyday life and our experience of Groundhog Day?

As men, we have the opportunity to invest in the lives of those around us, to care for people. They may be family, wife, kids or others. They may be friends, or work colleagues, or people in our community. If you're a follower of Jesus, they will certainly include those in the Christian community that you belong to—your whole church, as well as smaller groups within your church. It's the opportunity to invest our lives in the people who really matter to us.

I'm not sure who first said, "80 percent of life is just turning up", but they were right. One of the secrets to living life well is in deciding what is worth doing and who you should care for, and then continuing to just turn up and do it. For the man who follows Jesus, inevitably this will mean endurance and patience. Keep on doing it day after day, week after week, year after year. Life shouldn't be all about gritting your teeth and turning up, so I'll speak about having fun and being refreshed soon. But let's focus for now on getting the job done.

There's great power in just turning up, in committing to a person or a cause and following through on your commitment. Rarely do you make a real difference in one amazing incident or appearance; it's usually in the persistence of turning up. Endurance and patience are what it takes, and God promises that those who follow Jesus can have this through the work of his Spirit in their lives.

A great example of this was right in front of me as a kid, but I wasn't switched on enough to realize it until much later. My grandfather was the greatest example of endurance and patience I've ever seen.

Donald Shaw was born beside the Clarence River in northern New South Wales in 1891. In 1915, at the age of 24, he marched with a group of men from Grafton (on the Clarence) to Sydney (660 km) to volunteer to fight in World War I. The Australian Boomerang Regiment, as they were called, started with 27 men in Grafton and finished in Sydney with 240. They fought in France, where Donald was the victim of a gas attack. He recovered and came back to live in Grafton, where he became a genuine follower of Jesus at the age of 30 in the Free Presbyterian Church of Scotland. He married Eliza, and they had seven children (my mother was the youngest of these children, born in 1935). In that same year, as my grandfather attended church, the minister, the Reverend JP McQueen, announced that he was returning to Scotland. He also announced that Donald Shaw would be taking the church services until the new minister arrived. As far as I know, this was news to my grandfather. He hadn't been asked before the announcement was made. He was then 44 years old.

My grandfather was not highly educated, and so felt unable to preach or teach. So he would prepare published sermons from the great preachers of the past (men like Charles Spurgeon, George Whitfield and JC Ryle). He would then read these sermons beautifully in the church meetings. He would pray, and he would lead the singing. It was only a little church, but he would do it all. He generally did this twice on a Sunday, and at a midweek meeting. When he went on holidays, he would go to the beach at Yamba, near Grafton, so that on Saturday afternoon he could catch the bus back from the beach, take the church meetings on the Sunday, then go back to the beach again on Monday. When the church lawn needed mowing, he would ride his bicycle from one side of Grafton to the other while carrying the push mower in his hand, mow the lawn, and ride back home again. He did this week by week without fail, again and again, until the next minister arrived from Scotland.

The next minister arrived in 1972, 37 years later. My grandfather was then 81 years old.

Donald John Shaw died in 1983 at the age of 92. What did he really care about? What did he really believe? It was very obvious. He showed it with great *endurance* and *patience*. Did it make a difference? That little church is still going strong nearly 90 years after he was handed the job of covering the gap between ministers. In 2019 and 2020, three of his great-great-grand-children were baptized in that church. He just kept turning up; he kept doing what mattered to support those around him.

The challenge for us as men is this: who or what do we really value? So much of life is mundane, Groundhog-Day 'everyday-ness'. Again, and again, and again. But when we understand who it is for and what we really value, turning up again and again starts to feel different. We turn up, not passive or resigned or sulky or petulant, but deliberate and intentional. It's saying to yourself, "I will go to work; I will die the death of 10,000 com-mutes". It's saying, "I will take my kids to sport on a Saturday, even when I'm tired". Or, because you're a Christian, "I will choose to turn up at church even when I'm tired. I will make the effort to speak to the new people. I will be hospitable and invite people to my home. And I'll do this not to get in Jesus' good books, but because I am already loved by him, and I'm committed to the people in my church." Perhaps it means saying, "I will make time for old friends, even when it's not convenient", or "I will make the effort to make new friends". Or, if you're a single man, "I will use my extra freedom to care for people or to find a cause that I will invest in".

Why? Because that's what you do. You keep turning up to make a difference. And you keep doing it again, and again, and again. You keep turning up. You keep turning up.

In my own life, as I look at my meagre achievements, anything I've achieved has been through patience and endurance—through just turning up. I've been married 40 years. How do you achieve that? Day by day, you keep turning up. I've given approximately 4,000 Bible talks over 30 years. Has any single talk particularly stood out and been world changing? No. But, over years and years of just turning up, valuable things happen.

So here's my question to you: what will you keep turning up to? What is it, or who is it, that you will dedicate your life to? If you're a Christian, it'll mean serving Jesus. But how? Where will you keep showing up, not because you feel locked in or you have no choice, but because you know what's really valuable?

You still need to have fun; you need to do stuff that refreshes you—whether that's golf, or learning to cook, or deep-sea fishing, or whatever it is. In fact, I think if you're a married man you probably need to be working on some little project that your wife rolls her eyes at. Something that is just plain fun and refreshes you. My mate Peter runs ultramarathons. Other mates do the MAMIL thing (Middle-Aged Man in Lycra) and spend a few hours on a road bike. Once a year, I organize a hunting trip to Cape York. It's a chance to blow off some steam, and to come home physically exhausted but emotionally recharged.

Most of us will often feel like life is Groundhog Day, filled with a strange combination of boredom and stress. But knowing why you're doing it, and who you're doing it for, makes all the difference. Scottish author Robert Louis Stevenson said, "Everyday courage has few witnesses. But yours is no less noble because no drum beats for you, and no crowds shout your name."

Turning up day by day with endurance and patience may not be noticed by many others, but it has great value. If you're a follower of Jesus, there's an eternal value in this. The opportunity to invest in people, to live a life following Jesus, is not easy. But live that life consistently and you'll earn the opportunity to speak about him to people. You need to play the long game.

There's an episode of *The Simpsons* set earlier in their family life, when Homer and Marge only have two children, Bart and Lisa. Homer has the opportunity to live his dream of leaving his job at the nuclear power plant to work in the tenpin bowling alley. He loves it there, partly because he can put his head in the bowling ball shiner. Life is perfect. But then Marge becomes pregnant, and they realize they won't be able to survive financially with Homer's lower wage. And so Homer has to literally crawl back to Mr Burns at the nuclear power plant and take his old job back. Mr Burns makes him crawl through the pet door to his office. And to rub salt in the wound before giving Homer his job back, Mr Burns puts a sign on the wall in front of Homer's desk: "Don't forget: you're here forever". But the final scene of the episode shows Homer in one of his better moments—with pictures of his new daughter, Maggie, strategically placed on the wall to cover parts of the sign so that it now reads: "Do it for her". He understands why he's putting up with Groundhog Day, with a job that he doesn't love. He does it for her.

And that changes everything.

PART TWO

HEALTHY MASCULINITY LIVED OUT

In the first half of *The Manual*, we've looked at masculinity: its crisis and its critics, and why healthy masculinity is still so necessary and so good. But masculinity doesn't exist in a vacuum; it is lived out in relationships with other people.

The second half of this book deals with six key relationships for men, and what healthy masculinity will look like when it's lived out in these relationships day by day. I know not all men will have all six of these relationships, but together these are building blocks of a life well lived.

7. MAN UP AS A SON

Y OUR MATE LEANS across the table. Holding up his phone, he asks, "Can I show you a picture? Here he is. He's not very strong, almost walking, doesn't have many teeth, can't really look after himself; but he's really affectionate. We feed him his meals; soft food from a blender. He sleeps all the time. We dress him. He loves being taken on outings." Do you want to see the photo? If it's a picture of his baby son, it's all smiles and congratulations. If it's a picture of his elderly father, it's kind of weird. But the description of no teeth, not walking, and soft food might apply equally to both. What's going on? Why is one photo cute and the other weird?

We live in a strange society. We only seem able to look forward, while the rear-view mirror of life is out of focus or altogether absent.

To start writing this chapter on how to man up as a son, I did a Google search of 'books on family'. There are hundreds of books about how to be good parents and how to raise kids, but very few on how to be a good son (or daughter). Why? There's a different vibe in caring for parents. Our kids, if we have them, feel like an extension of us. Our investment in them is an investment in our future. But looking after our parents can often feel like we are looking back, perhaps paying back a debt rather than making an investment in the future. And we all know debt is never fun.

But let's man up and realize that, for almost all of us, there is a debt. There is a debt to previous generations for their work, their struggle, so that we aren't sitting in a cave somewhere, huddled in the dark and gnawing on tree roots. Jordan Peterson pushes his readers to remember what it cost previous generations, especially our parents, to give us the privileges we so easily take for granted:

> *To act to justify the suffering of your parents* is to remember all the sacrifices that all the others who lived before you (not least your parents) have made for you in all the course of the terrible past, to be grateful for all the progress that has been thereby made, and then to act in accordance with that remembrance and gratitude. People sacrificed immensely to bring about what we have now. In many cases, they literally died for it—and we should act with some respect for that fact.[1]

Our family of origin obviously has a huge effect on us, for good or for ill. No family is perfect. As my wife says, "Every family is dysfunctional in some way"—though some families punch way above their weight in this area. When my friend Walter was asked by his son, "What's a normal family, Dad?" he gave this answer: "Saying a family is normal is just a way of talking about people you don't know very well". And in our dysfunctional families, parents are caught up in the middle of it all. In this chapter, most of what I'll say can be applied to parents and children generally. But, sadly, there's often dysfunction between sons and fathers; in my experience, it's that relationship that can so often be uneasy.[2] Every young man I meet who is about to become a dad, or who has a new baby boy, is planning to have a great relationship with

---

1   Peterson, *12 Rules for Life*, p 360 (emphasis original).
2   I know sons and mothers can have dysfunctional relationships as well, but I'll leave that for now. If you want to think further on this, Jordan Peterson discusses the controlling mother; see *12 Rules for Life*, pp 320-332.

his son. This desire was obviously the same for fathers a generation or two ago, so why is it that so many relationships between fathers and sons are so strained?[3]

Part of the answer may be very simple: parenting is hard work. Growing up means realizing that our parents are simply fellow human beings who are stumbling along like the rest of us, and in most cases making it up as they go. It's this realization that will help you in relating to them with gratitude (and forgiveness where necessary). It's interesting how becoming a parent yourself switches on the lights about your own parents. You have no idea what's involved in parenting until it hits you. Bang! What just happened? The survival of the human race depends on the blissful ignorance of potential parents. Becoming a parent opens our eyes about our own parents and how tough it was raising us (perhaps this is one of the reasons why grandchildren are so special to grandparents). Having children of our own will help us appreciate our parents' efforts, or at least help us to be a bit more forgiving of them. In saying that, having our own kids isn't essential. Just growing up should make us more understanding and appreciative.

There are two things we should grasp about our parents.

Firstly, *gratitude*. Realizing how much they loved you, even if they weren't so good at showing it, is important. Appreciating how much it cost to raise you—in time, effort and opportunity cost—matters. In fact, part of growing up is appreciating how much we've been handed by those who went before us, rather than simply taking them for granted.

---

3   Steve Biddulph says that in his experience, out of every 100 men, 30 are not speaking with their fathers, 30 have prickly relationships with their fathers, 30 only speak to their fathers out of duty, and only 10 have fathers whom "they admire, enjoy, and feel deep support from. Who will remain close to them until the day they die" (Biddulph, *The New Manhood*, pp 20-21). Sadly, in my experience, Biddulph is basically on the money with this description.

Secondly, *being able to forgive*. This is a huge issue, so let's take a moment to explore it in some detail.[4]

Forgiving your dad

Forgiveness is a very big issue within families, sometimes particularly between a father and a son. I'd go so far as to say it's an ability to forgive that keeps a family functional. But so often if you scratch just a little of the veneer from extended families, you'll uncover someone who is not talking to someone else because they won't forgive something that's been done or said. Ironically, often the 'something' was so long ago that the real problem now is the years of ignoring each other rather than the original offending action.

For us as men, our fathers have a profound effect on us—for good or for ill. There are many changes in the relationship between father and son as a boy grows to manhood, such as dad letting his boy grow up, and the change in the balance of power within the relationship. But, as I've already mentioned, one of the biggest changes happens as a son realizes that his father is only human, a fellow traveller who is doing his best as a dad and, like the rest of us, making it up as he goes. He has all the weaknesses and flaws of the rest of humanity. This might seem to be stating the obvious, but once the penny drops it helps enormously in enabling us to forgive our dads for the times they let us down.

Steve Biddulph has a great chapter in *The New Manhood* where he addresses the problem of father-and-son alienation—whether that involves not speaking to one another at all, or just

---

4   For an excellent full-length treatment of the Bible's teaching on forgiveness, see C Brauns, *Unpacking Forgiveness: Biblical answers for complex questions and deep wounds*, Crossway, 2008. On the relationship between forgiveness and repentance, see especially chapter 11.

having awkward conversations whenever they see each other.[5] Biddulph says this will never be fixed until you've had the "put the dead cat on the table" conversation: the full and frank exchange with your dad where you talk about his successes and his failures as a father, and you tell him that you forgive him.

Biddulph is talking about "the ideal result" or "true reconciliation", and it's a great thing to desire. Indeed, it's worth some pain to achieve it. But in my experience, it's not always possible. It takes two to have a conversation like this, to meet in reconciliation. I don't want to sound defeatist, but realistically in some families, no matter how hard you personally try, there are things that can't be fixed. It may well be necessary to draw a line under what has happened in the past, decide that you will care for your parents in the right way regardless, and move on.

Even more importantly, I believe true reconciliation between fathers and sons—or between anyone, for that matter—is only really possible when people embrace the message of forgiveness in Jesus and so can truly forgive each other.

"Every one says forgiveness is a lovely idea, until they have something to forgive."[6] Why? Because it costs to forgive. When someone wrongs us, we have a kind of moral right to extract justice, to punish or hurt them back in some way. That may take many different forms—everything from gossip to physical violence—but it's the same idea: you've hurt me, so I'll hurt you back. Forgiveness is the costly decision to not seek retribution, but instead to absorb the wrong. This is not the same as pretending the event never happened, and it's not the same as saying there are no consequences. Where I grew up, the expression would be to 'suck it up': refusing to hurt the other person or punish them. It's very hard, and many people are not prepared to

---

5 Biddulph, *The New Manhood,* chapter 2.
6 CS Lewis, *Mere Christianity,* HarperOne, 2015, p 115.

do it. Yet as we stumble forward in life, plagued by either deliberate or unthinking selfishness, it's only through forgiveness that we can keep any long-term relationships. Those who won't forgive, or won't ask for forgiveness, end up alone.

One of Jesus' most beautiful and yet confronting teachings is generally known as 'The Parable of the Unforgiving Servant' (Matt 18:21-35). In this parable, in a way that only the master storyteller can, Jesus shows us that forgiveness is costly and ultimately undeserved, but that God in his great mercy forgives those who come to him and ask. The cost, the absorbing of the wrong done before God, is Jesus' death in our place, which pays the price of forgiveness. Now, forgiveness from God is free and full and available. The sting in the tail (or tale) is that this overwhelming generosity to the Christian (the one who trusts Jesus) must flow out to the way we treat other people. The Christian person must be ready to forgive and restore relationship with those who ask for forgiveness. The Christian person must be the one with the outstretched hand who offers forgiveness and reconciliation. Though it's not easy, the motivation comes from how God has treated us. Jesus says that to deny those who ask for forgiveness means we have not understood, and therefore should not expect, forgiveness from God (see Matt 6:14-15).[7]

---

7   When it comes to forgiveness, does the wrongdoer have to be repentant in order to be forgiven, or are we just meant to forgive anyone for anything at any time? Let me give some principles in the case of serious matters where people have been damaged.

God calls on the Christian to forgive in the way God has forgiven them (e.g. Col 3:13). God forgives us when we are repentant—that is, when we have turned around and asked for forgiveness. (I also understand that bringing us to that point is the gift of God.) Someone who has done serious wrong needs to be challenged and called to repentance, and should ask for forgiveness from the one they have damaged. The end point of forgiveness is reconciliation, the restoring of the relationship. This is not possible if the wrongdoer is not repentant and will not come back to ask for forgiveness.

So if the wrongdoer (in serious matters) is unrepentant, how does the injured person respond? Look at what Paul says in Romans 12:

Any healthy father–son relationship needs two things: a willingness to apologize for mistakes and ask for forgiveness, and a willingness to accept that apology and offer that forgiveness.

"Honour your father and mother ..."

Now, imagine for a moment that you have to work out ten rules for how the human race is to behave. Only ten, and they have to last a very long time—like they were chiselled in stone. I know this has already been done, but bear with me. Given that you have to be able to count these rules on your fingers, there's only room for one rule about family life. What should it be? Most people would probably say, "Parents, love and care for your children". It's the natural way that life tilts. There are countless books and courses on how to be a good parent and how to raise your children. People talk about their kids or show you photos of their kids, and it's polite to feign an interest. Parents naturally look forward as their kids grow; it's exciting to see them learn to walk, talk, start school, and take the whole journey toward adulthood.

But when God gave the Ten Commandments to Israel (as recorded in Exodus 20), there was just one commandment about family life, and it doesn't say "Look after your kids"; it says, "Honour your father and your mother, so that you may live long

Do not repay anyone evil for evil. Be careful to do what is right in the eyes of everyone. If it is possible, as far as it depends on you, live at peace with everyone. Do not take revenge, my dear friends, but leave room for God's wrath, for it is written: "It is mine to avenge; I will repay," says the Lord. On the contrary:
"If your enemy is hungry, feed him;
if he is thirsty, give him something to drink.
In doing this, you will heap burning coals on his head." (Rom 12:17-20)

In sum, the Christian is told not to take revenge and to leave the matter to the justice of God. They are to act in the wrongdoer's best interest—which will need some careful thought. (Of course, Romans 12 and Jesus' parable in Matthew 18 are about personal relationships; I've not dealt with the issue of wrongdoing and the law, which is covered in Romans 13.)

in the land the LORD your God is giving you" (Exod 20:12).

Why that command? There are many reasons, such as the good ordering of a society and of the family units within it. But one of the main reasons is obvious: we need to be reminded or instructed or *ordered* to do it. For some of us, it's perfectly natural; for others, it's not easy. It depends largely on what home life was like. But looking back, acknowledging our parents and the sacrifices they made and what we owe them, is important. This commandment was given to ancient Israel, but it is a template for how God wants people to live even now.

In the *Oxford Dictionary*, the word 'honour' means "Great respect, esteem, or deferential admiration felt towards a person or thing". Notice the commandment doesn't say "Honour them if they deserve it". The people of Israel were to honour their parents, full stop. This command was given to Israel so that they would live long in the promised land. They were to listen to what their parents taught them about God and his promises and about living God's way so that the nation of Israel would prosper. The commandment to honour parents is clearly repeated in the New Testament and passed on to all those who follow Jesus. Paul's letter to the Christians in Ephesus says, "Children, obey your parents in the Lord, for this is right. 'Honour your father and mother'—which is the first commandment with a promise—'so that it may go well with you and that you may enjoy long life on the earth'" (Eph 6:1-3).

What does it look like practically to honour parents? It means we must treat them with respect, care for them (we'll say more about this later), make time for them in person and with phone calls, and perhaps even help them financially. Often in families, it works out that parents help their kids. They fund their studies at school, TAFE[8] or university, or help them in getting that first

---

8   Technical and Further Education

house. But it may be that later in life the shoe shifts to the other foot and the 'kids' need to care for their parents financially. If your parents are on a pension of some sort, a little bit extra month by month can make a huge difference to how they live. If your parents aren't 'good with money', you may need to set some boundaries around financial help. Maybe that means offering a regular allowance, rather than a lump sum, to help with financial burdens. You may need to be the one who takes the lead in organizing with your siblings about how you can financially help your parents.

If you're a follower of Jesus, it's worth noting that Jesus is really strong on caring for financially needy parents, and he is scathing towards those who play legal games to avoid the obligation (see Mark 7:8-12). The apostle Paul also makes this a high priority: "Anyone who does not provide for their relatives, and especially for their own household, has denied the faith and is worse than an unbeliever" (1 Tim 5:8).

Look carefully at the quote from Ephesians 6 above and you'll notice that there are two commands: (1) children, obey your parents; and (2) honour your father and mother. There's no release date on the honour commandment. If your mum and dad are alive, they are to be honoured. But is this the same as obedience? Are you always supposed to 'do as you're told'?

It's worth clarifying the difference between these two commands. Paul has said two separate things; 'honour' and 'obey' are not the same. 'Obedience' means do as you are told, whereas 'honour' means to treat someone with respect and care. The obedience command is to young children.[9] This makes sense in the context of the letter as Paul is working his way through explain-

---

9   We know this by looking at verse 4 in Ephesians 6, which uses the same Greek word for 'children' (teknon) as verse 1. Verse 4 is clearly talking about raising younger children—parents don't 'bring up' their children once they're adults—which strongly suggests that verse 1 also refers to young children.

ing how a series of relationships should work. In a sense, it's a household list: husbands and wives; parents and children; masters and slaves. There is a time in a son's or daughter's life when the direct obligation to obey parents ceases, but the obligation to honour and care for one's mum and dad never expires.

Now, let me stick my neck out on this one. Different cultures need to hear different parts of these instructions. I'm going to make a comment on Asian culture, but before I do let me try to cover my butt by saying that I married into an Asian family over 40 years ago, and I'm still happily part of that family. I have many more Asian relatives than I have Anglo relatives, and I wasn't born into the family; I chose this.

In Asian cultures, the younger generations sometimes need to learn that while honour for parents never expires, strict obedience to them can stop when you are no longer a child. (While I've married into an Asian family, I'm also a boy from a rural town where almost everyone is from an Anglo background, and our Anglo culture needs a prod in a different direction. We could do better at honouring our parents.)

Where is that line between obedience and honour? I humbly suggest that it's somewhere around the time of becoming financially independent and no longer living under your parents' roof. If you're still financially dependent or living under their roof, the obligation to obedience still applies. At least let's say you need to adjust your lifestyle to meet their expectations. If that's unreasonable at your present age, then there's an obvious solution. You fill in the gaps.

By the way, living under your parents' roof and having them financially support you means you should be more than just reluctantly doing the minimum to be obedient; you should work hard to make it a positive experience for them to have you around.

Remember, this is a book written to men, not women. So let me speak directly to young (or maybe some not-so-young) men:

if you're approaching 30 years of age, it's probably time to move out of home. I know your mum loves you and does your washing, but it's time to grow up and move out. This will also change your relationship with your parents. Once you're living out of home, assuming your parents are still in good health and are mobile fellow adults, honouring them will probably just mean reasonably regular contact. It's not that hard to pick up the phone once a week and call. If you're living close enough, having dinner with your folks once a week will be a highlight for them. If you're married and have kids, you may not appreciate how much grandparents love to see the grandkids. The answer is, of course, a lot!

Then comes that middle part of life when you can be driven mad by your kids and your parents at the same time. Once that inevitable time comes and your parents are aging and becoming less independent or even frail, life and decisions can become a little more complicated. Here is where a decision to honour and care really matters. If the message we need to hear about how to be a son varies according to our culture, it's worth noting that it also varies according to life stage—both our own life stage and our parents' life stage. In particular, we could do better at honouring our elderly and aging parents.

Honouring aging parents

I vividly remember the first time I realized I'd become a 'senior citizen'. I was catching the bus near the Sydney CBD. I thought I was in good shape: I worked out at the gym, and I felt pretty fit. When I got on the bus, every seat was taken—50 people with that 'thousand-yard stare'. I decided I could stand for the 20-minute ride, no worries. But then as I looked around, I noticed a young guy about 19 or 20, dark hair, sitting beside his girlfriend.

And then it happened.

Our eyes met, and he began to stand. It was like one of those slow-mo movie scenes where the bodyguard dives in front of the gunman. I wanted to dive over and yell, "Noooooo!" but it was too late. He stood for me and politely offered me the seat beside his girlfriend. I couldn't refuse. It would have embarrassed him in front of 49 other people. And so I thanked him and sat down. I then took out my phone and sent a text to my sister: "So this is how it ends".

What a great thing for this young man to do; his parents had taught him well. He had decided that I was old enough to be his father (which I was), and he would honour me by giving me his seat. That is a young man to be well respected. I did make the mistake, however, of telling my colleague Peter about what had happened. Every time I spoke at an event for the next year, Peter would introduce me with this story about how I was now a senior citizen.

It's good to have a laugh about getting older, but the truth is that it's not easy to become a senior citizen, especially in a culture that glorifies youth the way ours does. As a society, we often do a poor job of caring for elderly parents, and for the elderly generally. Care for the aged costs money, and too often our own 'lifestyle' gets in the way of caring for or honouring the aged. Australia's 2019 Royal Commission into Aged Care Quality and Safety was a damning report on the way so many of the elderly in our society are not adequately cared for.[10]

Let me offer a few thoughts on caring for aging parents. Firstly, if possible, be proactive. It is necessary to arrange extra care for parents as their level of independence declines. The problem is that older people usually don't want to accept these

---

10 N Robinson, 'Aged Care Royal Commission report is enough to make reader weep', *The Australian*, 1 November 2019, accessed 16 November 2021 (theaustralian. com.au/nation/aged-care-royal-commission-report-is-enough-to-make-reader-weep/news-story/068faba3d741c73ac4237a99a61ca174).

changes until they're forced to. The most obvious example is downsizing the family home and dealing with the contents of that home. As people age, stairs and large yards or gardens become a problem. Downsizing will often be resisted, as everyone likes the familiar, the family home where (hopefully) there are lots of positive memories. And no-one wants to acknowledge they are 'on the final lap'. The problem is that to be able to downsize, older people need to be reasonably functional. And if you're still functional, why would you downsize? Unfortunately, when you can no longer function, it's really too late. Good luck with sorting out this problem!

Secondly, you'll need to somehow arrange who is doing what with siblings, if you have them. The time to have these conversations is before the day-to-day pressure is on. It's good to be able to have a calm, pre-emptive conversation about expectations around who is doing what and how and when. It may be necessary for you to step up and take leadership in the wider family—making decisions; urging other family members to pull their weight.

Thirdly, be aware of the impact on parents of facing their own mortality. At this stage of life, when inevitably we realize we will die, a faith in Jesus and his promise of the resurrection makes all the difference in how we face the future. It's also hard for many aging men to come to terms with a loss of power—both physical and relational—in their lives. The phone rings less and less each year; fewer people ask for help or advice. One of my mates speaks about 'Relevance Deficit Disorder', particularly for men who were successful in their careers or in other areas of life. It's a hard pill to swallow.

If your parents are Christian, it's important to help them maintain access to hearing the Bible read and taught, and to Christian fellowship, as they become less mobile. Help them to be involved in their church for as long as possible. We need to care for their spiritual health as well as their physical wellbeing.

And they will love it if you read the Bible and pray with them; it will be a highlight of their day.

If you're a follower of Jesus and your parents are not, the end of life approaching is a difficult time for them and a heartache for you. Attitudes can harden over a lifetime, but they can also soften when our own mortality stares us in the face. I have no clichés to offer, and I have my own heartache in this area. So pray that God will soften hearts and open ears, and pray for the courage to grasp the opportunity to have those significant conversations when the moment arises.

Fourthly, honour for parents is vital, but sometimes what parents want would put unreasonable burdens on family members or on other people in terms of time, finances or other types of inconvenience. To man up as a son will mean loving and honouring parents, often sacrificially, but sometimes it will mean putting boundaries in place for the benefit of everyone involved. You'll have to wisely balance responsibilities such as caring for other people in your family and managing your job. Sometimes, to man up means making firm decisions about what is desired versus what is actually needed and fair.

Finally, if you have your own kids, know that they are watching how you treat your parents. You have the opportunity to teach them many important life lessons. Obviously, you are teaching them how to treat aging parents, and it's not hard to see how we have skin in the game with what we model to our kids. You can model behaviour that demonstrates care and love for your parents, while also maintaining gentle but clear boundaries where necessary. Explain the inevitable frailty and mortality to your kids. Remember, when the time comes, they will choose your walking frame.

This whole book is a call to men to live with a healthy masculinity, and nowhere is this clearer than in how we treat our parents. Remember our definition: *Healthy masculinity is a willingness to take responsibility and use the power you have to care for and nurture those around you.* Most of us will have the opportunity and ability to honour our father and mother while they are still around. Honouring parents is about understanding the tragedy of life: over time, even the strongest and brightest of us become frail and the light fades away. To man up, honour our parents and help them face their own mortality is not just a duty but a privilege. What's more, it will also teach us about our own mortality and the need to "number our days".[11]

---

11 "Teach us to number our days, that we may gain a heart of wisdom" (Ps 90:12).

8. MAN UP AS A FRIEND

HOW MANY FRIENDS do you have? I have hundreds, although I'm not sure who they are, I don't know what to do with them, and I don't talk to them. But, apparently, they're my friends.

I'm talking, of course, about Facebook 'friends'. I don't really know how to use Facebook properly. These are people who have asked to be my friends, so sure, with a click of a button their wish is granted. And yet when I look at Facebook, which happens very occasionally, it seems like it's full of bored people talking about inane things with other bored people who give inane answers. We can now have hundreds of 'friends' with the click of a button, friendships that extend across cities and all over the world. But it's just possible that we've devalued the meaning of the word 'friend'.

And at the same time, loneliness is killing us. Study after study shows loneliness is on the rise in Western nations. In England, the USA and Australia, the percentage of single-person homes tripled in the 60 years up to 2006, from around 9 percent to around 27 percent.[1] Loneliness is considered by many in the medical world to be a public health crisis in the making.

Two important studies on loneliness were recently published in Australia. The first was the *Australian Loneliness Report*,

---

1   D De Vaus and S Richardson (eds), *Living Alone in Australia: Trends in sole living and characteristics of those who live alone* [occasional paper], Census Series #4, Academy of the Social Sciences in Australia, 2009, p 4, accessed 7 January 2022 (socialsciences.org.au/publications/occasional-paper-2009-cs4).

published by the Australian Psychology Society and Swinburne University in 2018.[2] It listed the following major findings:

- One in four Australians feels lonely.
- Many Australians—especially younger Australians—report anxiety about socializing.
- 30 percent of people don't feel part of a group of friends.
- Lonely Australians are in worse physical and mental health and are more likely to be depressed.

Several factors were listed among the reasons for growing loneliness. These included:

- *The way we work:* For some, long commutes take them out of their community. Others are asked to move across cities or interstate for work, removing them from their established communities. Then there's the growth in FIFO (fly in, fly out) work and working from home.
- *Changing family structures:* More and more people are living alone, and the family unit is continuing to decrease in size.
- *Our stage of life:* Loneliness affects people of all ages. While people over 65 are the least lonely, all other age groups are affected in roughly equal measure.
- *Social media:* Ironically, far from helping with feelings of loneliness, social media is linked to the rise of depression and anxiety, particularly among millennials.[3]

The second study is entitled *Is Australia Experiencing an Epidemic of Loneliness?* Commissioned by Relationships Australia, this report noted that overall levels of loneliness for men are

---

2   Australian Psychological Society and Swinburne University of Technology, *Australian Loneliness Report: A survey exploring the loneliness levels of Australians and the impact on their health and wellbeing*, APS and Swinburne University, 2018, accessed 7 January 2022 (psychweek.org.au/2018-archive/loneliness-study).

3   See, for example, JM Twenge, 'Have smartphones destroyed a generation?', *The Atlantic*, September 2017, accessed 7 January 2022 (theatlantic.com/magazine/archive/2017/09/has-the-smartphone-destroyed-a-generation/534198).

higher than women, but that women were more likely to admit they were lonely when it came to answering a survey question.[4] The study also found "the highest rates of loneliness were reported by younger men ... who were widowed, followed by divorced and separated men". In particular, men who were unemployed or on income-support benefits reported being very lonely.[5]

One English study estimated that the feeling of loneliness has the same effect on your health as smoking 15 cigarettes a day.[6] Loneliness is a problem across the Western world. It's considered such a problem in the UK that in 2018 the government created a new position: Minister for Loneliness. In Australia, we don't have a minister for loneliness, but we do have the Australian Coalition to End Loneliness, with faculty from many of our universities and not-for-profit community care organizations involved.

Of course, these studies were all done prior to COVID-19—the game changer. If loneliness was a problem before, you can imagine what social distancing and being told to stay in your home for weeks or months on end has done to the situation.

Where has this epidemic of loneliness come from? It's been creeping up on us for years. And as is so often the case, it's grown out of something good that's become twisted along the way.

Modern individualism and the value of friendship

The Western world is built on the concept of the individual. There are various theories about the precise origins of this con-

---

4   P Mance, *Is Australia experiencing an epidemic of loneliness? Findings from 16 waves of the Household Income and Labour Dynamics of Australia Survey* [working paper], Relationships Australia, 2018, accessed 7 January 2022 (relationships. org.au/document/is-australia-experiencing-an-epidemic-of-loneliness), p 21.
5   Mance, *Is Australia experiencing an epidemic of loneliness?*, p 23.
6   N Tate, 'Loneliness rivals obesity, smoking as health risk', *WebMD*, 4 May 2018, accessed 7 January 2022 (webmd.com/balance/news/20180504/loneliness-rivals-obesity-smoking-as-health-risk).

cept. In his book *Inventing the Individual*, Larry Siedentop put forward a case for the roots of the Western understanding of the individual being found in Christianity. In the ancient world, the Greco–Roman world, people didn't think of themselves as individuals, but as members of families. This way of thinking extended to include every aspect of their lives. They lived and died within their family. The head of the family, the *paterfamilias*, determined the whole family's religion and life choices, sometimes even holding the power of life and death.

It was the teaching of Jesus—that every individual is spiritually responsible for how he or she responds to their knowledge of God, and that he or she can make individual moral decisions—that created a revolution around the idea of the 'individual'. The apostle Paul further developed this concept and took it to the Gentile (non-Jewish) world. Siedentop's thesis is that this notion spread through the church, becoming more significant as bishops and other church leaders came to fill the authority gap that developed after the fall of the Roman Empire. It was through the church and church courts that the value of the individual was woven into the fabric of Western thought.

Regardless of where the idea of the 'individual' came from, the pendulum has now swung so far that 'individualism' dominates the way people in the Western world conceive of themselves. Life is now all about *me* and *my* passions and *my* dreams.

One of the consequences of individualism is that we individuals are very often alone. We all make up our own minds, live our own lives, and yet are desperately lonely. But at the risk of stating the obvious, we're hardwired to need relationships; we need people to connect with. The Bible starts with humanity being created "in the image of God", for relationship with God and with one another (Gen 1:26-27).

Even those who aren't followers of Jesus can see the vital importance of relationships. Sebastian Junger is a journalist who has written a number of books about war and men in extreme situations.[7] He made the documentary *Restrepo* after being embedded for a year in a frontline US army post in Afghanistan, where he lived cheek by jowl with soldiers in life-and-death situations. His book *Tribe* is about the desperate need that all people, but particularly men, have to connect with one another, to feel part of a tribe. He says:

> [A]s society modernized, people found themselves able to live independently from any communal group. A person living in a modern city or suburb can, for the first time in history, go through an entire day—or an entire life—mostly encountering complete strangers. They can be surrounded by others and yet feel deeply, dangerously alone.[8]

> Whatever the technological advances of modern society—and they're nearly miraculous—the individualized lifestyles that those technologies spawn seem to be deeply brutalizing to the human spirit.[9]

Junger argues persuasively that disasters or extreme situations like war can actually lift morale and mental health. How? They smash individualism and make people bond as the pressure of life grows. This increases relational and emotional satisfaction among people, regardless of the suffering or disruption. Junger refers to Charles Fritz and his book *Disasters and Mental Health*:

> Disasters, [Fritz] proposed, create a "community of sufferers" that allows individuals to experience an immensely reassuring connection to others. As people come together

---

7   Junger has said publicly he is an atheist; see B Dunn, *Sebastian Junger*, Freedom from Religion Foundation website, n.d., accessed 7 January 2022 (ffrf.org/news/day/17/01/freethought/#sebastian-junger).
8   S Junger, *Tribe: On homecoming and belonging*, Twelve, 2016, p 18.
9   Junger, *Tribe*, p 93.

to face an external threat, Fritz found, class differences are temporarily erased, income disparities become irrelevant, race is overlooked, and individuals are assessed simply by what they are willing to do for the group. It is a kind of fleeting social utopia that, Fritz felt, is enormously gratifying to the average person and downright therapeutic to people suffering from mental illness.[10]

What people miss, presumably, isn't danger or loss, but the unity that these things often engender. These events bring stress on each person in a group, but there may be even greater stressors on a person in isolation. Counterintuitively, during disasters there is a net gain in wellbeing. Junger's point is that it's the bond of relationship that really matters to us in life, even to the point where being in the middle of disaster actually improves our lives because it brings us closer to each other.

The ancient world recognized the importance of friendship in a way that our modern world doesn't. We need friendship, yet we don't seem to prioritize it. In his book *The Four Loves*, CS Lewis wrote extensively about the value of friendship:

> To the ancients, friendship seemed the happiest and most fully human of all loves; the crown of life and the school of virtue. The modern world, in comparison, ignores it. We admit of course that besides a wife and family a man needs a few 'friends'. But ... it is something quite marginal; not a main course in life's banquet; a diversion; something that fills up the chinks of one's time. How has this come about?[11]

I turned 62 last year, and so I've been thinking about my life, what really matters, and what has real value. Of course, my faith in Jesus is central. Then Kathy, my wife of 40 years, and four kids

10   Junger, *Tribe*, pp 53-54.
11   CS Lewis, *The Four Loves*, Geoffrey Bles, 1960, p 55.

and three grandkids are central to my life. My family has brought me enormous joy, and some heartache. But as I think on what else truly matters, it's the friendships that I've had—and that I have. I have friends who've been around for—well, I think in decades—a decade, two decades, three or four decades, and some for just a few years. These friendships have been at the centre of my life and have been invaluable.

The *Oxford Dictionary* defines a friend as "a person with whom one has a bond of mutual affection, typically one exclusive of sexual or family relations". Some would say that friends are God's apology for giving you relatives. Depending on your family and friends, you may or may not agree with that. But I hope you would agree that life is about relationships. Get the relationships right, and life will be right. It's about people and what we share with them. And you know that it's true. Doing things alone is just not the same. Sharing something with someone more than doubles it. In fact, the whole nature of friendship is "seeing something together", sharing something significant. CS Lewis explains it like this:

> Friendship arises out of mere companionship when two or more of the companions discover that they have in common some insight or interest or even taste which the others do not share and which, till that moment, each believed to be his own unique treasure [or burden]. The typical expression of opening friendship would be something like, "What? You too? I thought I was the only one."[12]

Here's how psychologist Martin Seligman puts it:

> When asked what, in two words or fewer, positive psychology is about, Christopher Peterson, one of its founders, replied, *"Other people"*.

---

12 Lewis, *The Four Loves*, pp 61-62.

Very little that is positive is solitary. When was the last time you laughed uproariously? The last time you felt indescribable joy? The last time you sensed profound meaning and purpose? The last time you felt enormously proud of an accomplishment? Even without knowing the particulars of these high points of your life, I know their form: all of them took place around other people.

Other people are the best antidote to the downs of life and the single most reliable up.[13]

Life is just not the same on your own. To hit the hole in one, catch the big fish, go to the greatest concert, shoot the best feral pig, or ride your fastest lap time, or maybe even to drink that cappuccino as a MAMIL (Middle-Aged Man in Lycra)—these are just not the same when experienced alone. Even work relies on those around us. You can be at work and doing a difficult, tiring and boring job, but if you're doing it with your mates, if there's camaraderie, it's very different.

So, if you find it hard to make friends, you need to find stuff to do with other blokes. If you look for friendship as such, it's hard to find without it being in the context of sharing things with other men. It's not wrong to focus on trying to find friends, and to be deliberate about making and keeping friends. It just helps if there is a context of shared experience.

Often, we men don't understand friendship that well, or we're not intentional about it. In his book *The Buddy System*, Geoffrey Greif shares the results of his detailed research with 400 men in the USA—men from all different classes and racial backgrounds. His findings are reasonably predictable—the whole book feels a little like the guy who borrows your watch then tells you the

---

13 M Seligman, *Flourish: A new understanding of happiness and well-being—and how to achieve them*, Free Press, 2011, p 20.

time—but he does offer some good summaries. For example, what makes a friend?

- Being understood
- Trust and loyalty
- Dependability
- Doing things together (forgive the generalization, but men do things shoulder-to-shoulder, whereas women's friendships tend to be face-to-face)
- Commonality—things such as race, religion, age and class.[14]

I'd add one more. A friend is someone who will tell you hard things because they care for you. It's your friends who'll tell you what you need to hear. "Wounds from a friend can be trusted, but an enemy multiplies kisses." (Prov 27:6)

Greif goes on to explain some of the key differences between men's friendships and women's friendships:

> For example, men do not show as much physical affection or offer as many compliments to each other as do women. They do not require as much or as intense verbal communication from their male friends. Men compete more openly than women, and do so by following pre-set rules in that competition, like those established in sports.[15]

The costs and challenges of friendship

We value friendship. And yet as the research and life experience show, many men don't have a lot of friends. What gets in the way of making or keeping friends? Greif highlights the work of social scientist Robert Lewis, who gives four possible reasons:

14 GL Greif, *Buddy System: Understanding male friendships*, Oxford University Press, New York, 2009, p 46.
15 Greif, *Buddy System*, p 20.

First, [men's] friendships are maintained at a physical and emotional distance because men fear emotional and physical closeness, which they link to homosexuality. Second, adult role models are lacking—because their fathers did not have many friends, today's men do not learn how to make friends from them. ... The third and fourth reasons are a fear of being vulnerable and competition between men. If we add to these four a fifth reason—that men are taught to control their emotions—then the opportunities to connect with other men are greatly restricted.[16]

To maintain any relationship, there's a cost. In fact, all relationships involve sacrifice to some extent. What's necessary to maintain men's friendships? My theory is that there are two main requirements, two big prices to be paid, for men to hold on to friends.

Cost 1: Time

The first cost is time. To form and keep friendships, men need to make time—sometimes spontaneously, sometimes in the diary.

Planned time

You may think you're too busy to have or to maintain friendships at this stage of your life. Maybe your career is too pressured, or there are just too many demands on your time. If you think these things, give yourself an uppercut and keep reading.

A friend of mine used to serve as Chief of Staff for the Premier of New South Wales.[17] Speaking at a men's event, my friend said he was looking to the future and expecting that at some stage he would suffer from 'Relevance Deficit Disorder', where you aren't that important anymore and the phone doesn't ring so much. It

16 Greif, *Buddy System*, p 36.
17 A state premier in Australia is similar to the governor of a state in the USA.

was an important insight. We'll all suffer from Relevance Deficit Disorder someday. In fact, there'll come a time when we're actually looking for emails or hoping the phone will ring. If you're busy, there's a great temptation to think you don't have time for people—for friends. But be assured that Relevance Deficit Disorder *will* arrive, and it's your family and friends, the people you've shared your life with, who will get you through.

So make time. Keep in touch with mates. Long-term friendships are gold. Do stuff together, and plan it in advance; note it in your diary or calendar. If you're married, explain to your wife that time with your mates will make for a happier husband who is much easier to live with.

As life circumstances change, being intentional about time with mates becomes even more important. Changes in things like marital status or job location will mean we need to be deliberate about keeping in touch and having time for friends. There's also the cost of welcoming new friends, of making time, of putting in the effort to get to know people. We should pay this cost partly just because we value other people.

When it comes to friendship, the relationship is more important than the task or activity that you do together. There's one man I know who wants to go fishing, but will only go fishing in the middle of the night in winter because "that's when the fish bite". He hasn't really understood that the point of going fishing with a mate is spending that time together. Surprise, surprise, no-one wants to go fishing with him anymore.

One of the key secrets to life is understanding that, whether it's sport or exercise or a concert or whatever, the opportunity for togetherness is more important than the activity. If we fail to learn this, our friendships will only ever be an inch deep. If we are selfish in relationships, especially with time, we'll end up alone.

Unplanned time

Of course, the time when friends really need you, the key moments, are rarely planned. Things just happen in life. So we'd better have our eyes open to see what really matters in the moment.

I remember a time when I failed at this very badly. I've lived in half-a-dozen houses in the past 30 years and had 20 or 30 sets of neighbours, so this will be totally anonymous. It was a Wednesday night in July, and the State of Origin was about to start.[18] A couple of mates had come around to watch the game on TV, and kick-off was a couple of minutes away. Over the noise of the TV and the sporting clichés, I heard a noise: raised voices on the driveway next door. I walked outside to have a quick look. My neighbour, Tom[19] (a man I had known and liked for years), was standing in his driveway next to my house looking shattered. "What's the matter, mate?" I asked. He explained slowly and sadly that he'd had a major blow-up with his wife. It hadn't ended well—she had driven off, and it was really serious (in fact, later it was to mean the end of their marriage). I half-listened as he told me the story of his life unravelling—but only half, because kick-off was happening and the game was starting. Eventually I muttered some clichés expressing my concern, then went back inside to watch the game. My neighbour's marriage never recovered, and I've felt guilty for many years when I think of that night.

It's not that I have a messiah complex and assume I could have fixed it. It's just that I so totally got the 'time' wrong. I can't remember the result of that game. I can't even remember who was there to watch it with me. I don't know if my neighbour remembers the incident, but I remember it, and I know I made a massive mistake in not understanding time and friendship. I

---

18 For those not in Australia, the State of Origin is a major rugby league game between Queensland and New South Wales.
19 Not his real name.

didn't understand the need to give my friend the time—unscheduled, inconvenient, relational time—that he needed. I didn't do the right thing. I got it completely wrong.

When friends really need our time, it's rarely convenient, but it's worth thinking about it this way: "I may be under pressure to do *x*, but will I remember what I'm rushing off to do in a month, or six months, or a year?" Almost certainly the answer is no, but I guarantee the friend (or potential friend) who needs a listening ear, or help of some kind, will remember it in a year, two years, and maybe for a lot longer.

Cost 2: Forgiveness

The second cost of having friends is forgiveness. I had plenty to say about this idea in the previous chapter, but it's worth mentioning again here. In the context of friendship, forgiveness might mean putting up with the inevitable things your friends do that annoy you, or it might mean forgiving a big mistake when someone lets you down and hurts you badly.

For example, competitiveness between men is a good thing. There's a lot of fun to be had in playing different sports, or enjoying other forms of competition together. "Iron sharpens iron, and one man sharpens another" (Prov 27:17, HCSB). But there's a competitive line that can be crossed, and those who always want to compete and show that they're bigger, better, faster, smarter, or whatever—they can quickly become annoying. If you want to have friends, sometimes it's necessary just to be patient and let it slide. And to take it one step further, there are blokes who you know will inevitably let you down, whether that be by deliberately doing something that annoys you or unthinkingly hurting your feelings or letting you down. If you're not prepared to forgive people, you'll end up with very few friends.

Maintaining friendship

In different stages of life, there are different pressures on friendship. When you're single, at school or university, or even in the first few years of work, it's much easier. There's lots of free time, and it's easy to keep up with your mates. If you marry, there's the challenge of getting to know your wife's friends and potentially building friendships with other couples. But it is still a good thing to have mates who are just your mates, and who give you the opportunity for all-male friendship. You will need to negotiate this with your wife.

Once children come on the scene, most of life goes into survival mode for a while, and it will be necessary to be very intentional about keeping up with mates. Middle age means job pressures, tiredness, continued pressure with family, teenagers and driving kids to their activities. Once again, you'll need to be intentional. In old age—well, one of the inevitabilities of old age is that friendships start ending. Your mates start dying, and it's necessary to be deliberate and to use what energy you have to keep up with old friends and to make new friends, or you will end up in a diminishing circle. I suppose what this means is that at every stage of life, from finishing school right through to the nursing home, we need to be deliberate, allocate time, and be willing to forgive in order to maintain friendships.

Why is it so important to *maintain* friendships? Old friendships are very special. There is nothing quite like lives that have been lived out together. I have had some friendships for over 40 years. That's a lot of shared history. And it's often inconvenient to maintain those friendships. Our cohort at Bible college has a reunion every year. Last year, we clocked over our 30th year of meeting together for two or three days after Easter. It's never convenient to go, and I stress about how much else I have on my plate, but I always come home saying, "That was worth the effort, and we must keep on getting together".

My son has been out of school for about 12 years. He still gets together once a year with his schoolmates for a weekend away. This is a great thing for him to do and will stand him in good stead over the years. But, once again, it needs to be deliberate.

Friendship and the Bible

The Bible is very positive about friendships. For example, the right friends will help us to be the best men we can be. As we just saw, "Iron sharpens iron, and one man sharpens another" (Prov 27:17, HCSB). Good friends will also listen carefully when you have something serious to talk about: "Perfume and incense bring joy to the heart, and the pleasantness of a friend springs from their heartfelt advice" (Prov 27:9).

Friendships make a huge difference as we face the hard things in life. The book of Ecclesiastes puts it this way: "Two are better than one, because they have a good return for their labour" (Eccl 4:9). It also says, "if two lie down together, they will keep warm. But how can one keep warm alone?" (Eccl 4:11). This second verse may not seem particularly appealing as you consider your male friends. But believe me, if you're stuck in the bush or in the freezing cold, keeping warm could be very important. I've spent a night alone in the bush with a bogged vehicle and huddled up to a Rhodesian Ridgeback trying to keep warm. Another human being would have smelled better.

One of Jesus' most fascinating teachings is about friendship. The New Testament records that Jesus claims to be God-become-man—to be God, and yet one of us. He backs up these claims, too. The power of his teaching, the miracles he performed, and the fact that he rose from the dead all powerfully back up his claim to deity. And yet Jesus, the God–man, calls his followers his *friends*. To be a Christian is to be a friend of Jesus. He's still our Lord and master; but, incredibly, he's also our friend. And Jesus is the ultimate friend: "Greater love has no-one than this: to lay down one's life for one's friends" (John 15:13).

We've already seen that real friendship is costly. Jesus offers us friendship with himself. But did you notice the cost for Jesus? He lays down his life for his friends—to pay the price required for our forgiveness.

But there's also a cost in the response that he calls his friends to make: "You are my friends if you do what I command" (John 15:14). It's not so much that we earn his friendship, but that friendship requires trust, and trust will mean listening to what he says and doing what he commands.

And so what has changed? "I no longer call you servants, because a servant does not know his master's business. Instead, I have called you friends, for everything that I learned from my Father I have made known to you" (John 15:15).

Friendship means knowing Jesus' business, knowing his priorities and plans, in a way that the servant doesn't. Remember, he says this in the context of spelling it all out on the night before he's crucified. But even more than that, Jesus refers to his followers as his brothers—those who have the same father:

> Both the one who makes people holy and those who are made holy are of the same family. So Jesus is not ashamed to call them brothers and sisters. He says,
>
> > "I will declare your name to my brothers and sisters;
> >   in the assembly I will sing your praises."
> > (Heb 2:11-12)

Christians generally, and Christian men, are to think of each other as brothers having the same father, with Jesus as an older brother. We're brothers who are on a mission together with a job to do; with something to unite us. Perhaps Sebastian Junger is right when he describes our natural longing to be part of a band of brothers, with a mission that brings unity.[20] The New Testament is very strong on the need to care for one another, to welcome new men, to encourage each other, to put hope in the heart and steel in the spine of those other men who follow Jesus: "We know that we have passed from death to life, because we love each other" (1 John 3:14). Those who follow Jesus need to be deliberate about friendship. Carve out time for friends—sometimes spontaneous, often planned. And remember the need to forgive and be patient. Let's man up and care for our mates.

20 See Junger, *Tribe*, pp 71-103.

9. MAN UP AS A WORKMATE

AT 21 YEARS OF AGE, I was the assistant to the National Sales Manager of a transport company. He was only in his 30s, a high flyer, and sharp as a razor. For some reason he'd taken a shine to me. I'd only been his assistant for a few months when one day he called me into his office, leaned back in his big chair, looked at me with a smile, and told me a very politically incorrect parable—one that I can no longer repeat. But in his own, less-than-subtle way, he wanted to give me an important piece of advice. In essence, his point was that *everyone has a price*. "If you're going to sell your soul to the company, Alan, make sure you get a good price for it".

In today's workforce, there's probably less chance of 'selling your soul' to a particular company, simply because people change jobs so often these days. But perhaps you're tempted to sell your soul to your career in a more general sense. Do you think that's where you'll find meaning in life?

Then again, for some men, overcommitting to work is the last thing they'd ever do. Some of us just hang out for the weekend and do the minimum necessary at work to get through the week.

There are so many variations when it comes to men and work, where can I start? There are tradies and office workers, hi-vis, scrubs and suits. Skilled and unskilled. Higher up or lower down in the food chain. Running your own business or working for someone else. With so many variations in our experience of work, is there anything that can be said that's relevant and meaningful to men everywhere? Yep, absolutely.

We've said earlier that to man up or live with *healthy masculinity* is about a *willingness to take responsibility and use the power you have to care for and nurture those around you.* That's pretty obvious at home and within your family. But it doesn't stop when you go to work.

The five principles below are simple, really; they're about people and relationships being what matters. What's more, these principles are important because you need to play the long game at work. Just recently I gave my son a ride home. He's just over 30, and he's been working long hours over the last few months. He said with a sigh, "Dad, I'm really tired, and I've got 30 years to go". All I could think to say was "Yes mate, it's hard". I also thought (but didn't say), "It's tiring, and that's why they call it work and that's why they give you money for turning up". What does 35 or more years of it do to you? I see it every morning when I look in the bathroom mirror. It's called 'work' for a reason.

For some of us, there are maybe 40 years ahead in the workforce. What are some foundations you can hold on to as a man? If you're going to work for so long, you'd better work out what really matters—you'd better learn to play the long game. How do you do that? It starts with speaking the truth.

1. Tell the truth

It may seem like common sense, but a commitment to telling the truth to people means you can walk with your back straight and you needn't be afraid of things coming back to bite you. Tell the truth and you can always answer your phone, even for an unknown number. This is one of the drums Jordan Peterson keeps banging. And he's right. "Tell the truth—or, at least, don't lie" is his eighth rule for life. He says:

> Taking the easy way out or telling the truth—those are not merely two different choices. They are different pathways through life. They are ultimately different ways of existing.[1]

Lying easily becomes a habit, and it affects your character development:

> If you betray yourself, if you say untrue things, if you act out a lie, you weaken your character. If you have a weak character, then adversity will mow you down when it appears, as it will inevitably. You will hide, but there will be no place left to hide. And then you'll find yourself doing terrible things.[2]

When I worked at that transport company in my early 20s, one of the sales managers had the reputation of having a very casual relationship with the truth—that is, he was a liar. Everyone in the company knew this about him. Whether this was true or not was hard to know, but a reputation like this is very hard to get away from.

The book of Proverbs says a lot about truth and lies. For example, lying is a very short-sighted strategy in life; it will always come back to bite you. Telling the truth, on the other hand, is playing the long game: "Truthful lips endure forever, but a lying tongue lasts only a moment" (Prov 12:19). Tell the truth, and you never have to look over your shoulder: "An honest answer is like a kiss on the lips" (Prov 24:26).

2. Treat people with respect

In any organization there are those who wrongly are treated like they are invisible—people like the cleaners, the maintenance

---

1 Peterson, *12 Rules for Life,* p 209.
2 Peterson, *12 Rules for Life,* p 212.

workers or the doormen. Regardless of where you and they fit in the inevitable food chain, get to know them. Treat them with respect. The apostle Paul has some good advice here:

> Live in harmony with one another. Do not be proud, but be willing to associate with people of low position. Do not be conceited. (Rom 12:16)

Respect will mean treating people as more than just their job descriptions or functions. Treat them as complete human beings and take an interest in their lives.

Never assume because someone has a boring or poorly paid job that they are stupid or lazy or a failure. You can't know who people are by simply looking at them. When you ride in a taxi, ask the driver a little about himself or herself. It's surprising how often they have a PhD in rocket science from a non-English-speaking country, or they're a geophysics engineer or something similar, and they've come to your country to find a better life for themselves and their kids. Everyone has something to show us or teach us, if only we take the time to listen.

What's more, the people without the big titles and the big pay cheques generally run the place. They're the gatekeepers, the organizers; they have the keys; they make things happen. Learn their names, give them time, treat everyone with respect—not just because that's how you get things done, but because people deserve respect: they're made in the image of their Creator (Gen 1:27).

a. Treat women with respect

It shouldn't need to be said, but I'll say it anyway: always treat women with respect. I know there's confusion about how you're supposed to treat women in different contexts. I never know if I'm supposed to shake hands with a woman when I meet her. Now I just wait to see if her hand reaches out. If yes, I shake hands. If not, big smile and hello. How do you treat a woman with respect? It's not that hard to work out: simply treat women the way you would want someone to treat your sister or your wife or your mum at work. This is the gist of the apostle Paul's advice to his young lieutenant Timothy about how a Christian man should act towards members of the opposite sex: "Treat … older women as mothers, and younger women as sisters, with absolute purity" (1 Tim 5:1-2). Be polite, friendly and respectful, treating them exactly as you would if their husband or son or personal bodyguard were standing with them.

b. Treat those who are absent with respect

What I mean here is don't gossip. Stephen Covey was spot-on in *The 8th Habit*, his sequel to *The 7 Habits of Highly Effective People*, when he said:

> *Being loyal to those not present* is one of the most difficult of all the deposits.[3] It is one of the highest tests of both character and the depth of bonding that has taken place in a relationship. This is particularly the case when everyone seems to be joining in on bad-mouthing and piling on someone who is not present. You can, in an unself-righteous way, just speak up and say "I see it differently," or "My experience is different," or "You may have a point; let's go talk to him or her about it." By doing so, you instantly communicate that integrity is loyalty—not just to those absent but also to those who are present. Whether they acknowledge it or not, all the people present will inwardly admire and respect you. They will know that their name is precious with you when they're not there. On the other hand, when loyalty is a higher value than integrity in that you give in, go

---

3   Covey is talking about making 'deposits' of relational trust with people that demonstrate character and trustworthiness. Hence the title of the chapter: 'The voice and speed of trust'.

along, and join in the bad-mouthing, so, too, will everyone present know that under pressure and stress, you would do the same regarding them."[4]

Not surprisingly, the book of Proverbs has much to say about gossip and the damage it does. For one thing, it's not easy to resist gossip. Those poison words can actually seem sweet at the time: "The words of a gossip are like choice morsels; they go down to the inmost parts (Prov 26:22). But remember, when someone begins a sentence with "I shouldn't really tell you this, but …", be very careful what you trust them with. "A gossip betrays a confidence, but a trustworthy person keeps a secret" (Prov 11:13). And another simple rule for life: beware the person who talks too much; not only does it get boring, but they'll often be filling space with the wrong words: "A gossip betrays a confidence; so avoid anyone who talks too much" (Prov 20:19).

By the way, I'll finish with something my dad taught me, and which Stephen Covey hints at in the comment above: "If someone will gossip to you, they'll gossip about you."

Keep your eyes and your ears open. You'll soon work out who you can trust.

3. Don't sell your soul—remember it's relationships that will last

You need to have a life outside of work time. In my brief years in the corporate world, I saw many men who had sold their souls to the company. It hadn't been one big decision, but a thousand smaller decisions about priorities over the course of many years. The biggest sign of the sale was that they stayed at work much longer than necessary because there was nothing left to go home to.

4   S Covey, *The 8th Habit: From effectiveness to greatness*, Free Press, 2004, p 174 (emphasis original).

Sometimes, the call to sell your soul is clear and blatant. Lisa Pryor tells the story of a senior and very successful banker speaking about what's required to make it to the top of the industry:

> Assembled before him inside the silver skyscraper in London were a couple of hundred young bankers, associates in their twenties only a few years out of university, ready to be rallied and pepped, regaled with tales about the exciting future they could look forward to if only they followed in his footsteps. "Imagine that your life is like burners on a stovetop," he told them. Filling out the metaphor a little more, he explained that life consisted of four burners: work, family, friends and health. He came to his point: "To be a *good* banker, you need to turn off one burner." He paused for dramatic effect. "To be a *great* banker, you need to turn off two."[5]

Family, friends and health—would you cut out two of those to get to the top? I'm not saying don't work hard, and I'm not saying don't be ambitious. But have your eyes open to the cost or the direction of little compromises and where they are leading. You need to keep the big picture in mind, the compass of your life functioning, so you can see whether those little decisions are taking you in the direction you want to go.

As I mentioned earlier, if you're a millennial you're probably not considering selling your soul to a particular company. When I started in the workforce, it used to be that staying with one company long-term showed you were stable and reliable. Now, spending too long in one company can show you're risk-averse and you lack a wide experience. I recently spoke to a young woman who works for a top consulting firm; she told me that each employee gets a review every six months with "promote or dismiss" on the agenda.

---

5   L Pryor, *The Pinstriped Prison: How overachievers get trapped in corporate jobs they hate*, Picador, 2008, p 2 (emphasis original).

If you're a recent university graduate or you're yet to start full-time work, you may be expecting that your career will be the thing that gives your life meaning and purpose; work will be your passion and a great adventure. In this regard, the TED Talk stage and podcasts don't do us any favours—speakers who deliver brilliant presentations on how they have managed to get into careers they love, talking about how they're saving the planet while earning millions and loving every moment pursuing their passion.

I don't mean to be a wet blanket—actually, on second thought, that's exactly what I mean to be. I want you to remember that the reason people end up on the TED Talk stage is because they are very different from the average, and they have a unique story. You don't get invited onto the TED Talk stage if you've gone to work, done a standard job, worked hard, been paid an honest wage, and been average. Why? Because there's a lot of average people, and for average people work is work, and it won't deliver meaning to your life. The Bible says if you can enjoy your work, that's a gift from God.[6] But don't expect it to be the meaning of life, or you'll be disappointed.

4. Remember—there's a time coming when the phone won't ring anymore

English philosopher Alain de Botton is spot-on when he says that we all want "the love of the world around us".[7] You can call that love, or respect, or status. Call it what you want, but it's oxygen to a man's soul. Unfortunately, it's often easier for many men to get that respect or status at work than to get it at home. Perhaps it's tougher to earn it at home because those at home really know

---

6 "Moreover, when God gives someone wealth and possessions, and the ability to enjoy them, to accept their lot and be happy in their toil—this is a gift of God" (Eccl 5:19).
7 A de Botton, *Status Anxiety*, Penguin, 2005, p 1.

you. So it's easy to be caught up in the business of work and for work to take over our lives, not simply for the money (that's just a badge of playing and winning the game). Work can take over our lives because we enjoy the challenge, the achievement and the status that come with being the 'can-do' man.

In the early 1990s, I was the chaplain to the Sydney City Roosters rugby league team. That gave me the privilege of meeting Jack Gibson, then manager of the team and my boyhood hero. Jack was one of the greatest coaches the game has ever seen, and a commentator with a renowned dry wit that often left the audience laughing out loud. He was a legend of the game I had grown up loving. As the chaplain, I was a nobody at the club. Yet Jack Gibson treated me very well.

One winter's night, as the team trained at Henson Park in Sydney's inner west, Jack Gibson spoke to me across the fence that surrounded the oval. He told me, "When I was State of Origin coach in 1989 and 1990, the phone rang eighty times a day with journalists wanting to talk to me. But now the phone doesn't ring so much. So you'd better get used to the idea that the day will come when the phone doesn't ring anymore." It's the case for a lot of men. Work takes up their whole life, or so much of their life that when they retire they realize they have no friends and no interests outside work. And they're suddenly afflicted by that condition I mentioned earlier: Relevance Deficit Disorder.

Bettina Arndt quotes Roger Patulny, a sociology lecturer at the University of Wollongong, who analysed data on social contact in old age:

> Men are hit pretty hard by retirement because they haven't really had the opportunity to diversify their social networks as much (as their wives) and then find themselves devoid of the one network they have constantly relied upon for years.[8]

8   B Arndt, *#MenToo*, Wilkinson Publishing, 2018, p 268.

Arndt goes on to quote men's health expert Steve Carroll:

> "For many men, the problem is the lack of real relationships. While they have a working life they have plenty of social contact, superficial banter with their work mates, although it is striking how rarely they actually see their work companions outside of work. But when they retire they lose their major source of social contact and they become increasingly dependent on their wives."[9]

As strange as it may seem right now, there will come a time when you'll wish the phone would ring, and you may even be longing for emails. If you haven't invested in relationships, friends, family, some meaningful form of Christian service, and interests outside of work, it's going to be a very quiet retirement.

5. Be clear about who you are really working for

Unlike the philosophies of the Greeks and Romans in the ancient world, the Bible values work. Work is actually part of the way in which we can 'love our neighbours'. The Bible tells us that when God himself lived among us he spent years working as a carpenter (Mark 6:3). The vast majority of jobs are (by definition) about actually bringing benefit to someone. If it's not benefiting anyone, why would someone pay you to do it? So whatever your job, or wherever it fits into the 'food chain' that our world creates, it has value.

Ironically, the way the status food chain functions is in most cases completely wrong. The jobs wrongly seen as being at the bottom are so often the ones responsible for public health and the essential functioning of our society. If you're a follower of Jesus, as you work you're 'loving your neighbour', but you're also serving your Lord. The slave–master relationship in the ancient

9   Arndt, *#MenToo*, p 271.

world isn't an exact parallel to today's workplace, but it's close enough to draw out the principles.

The apostle Paul gives this instruction:

> Slaves, obey your earthly masters in everything; and do it, not only when their eye is on you and to curry their favour, but with sincerity of heart and reverence for the Lord. Whatever you do, work at it with all your heart, as working for the Lord, not for human masters, since you know that you will receive an inheritance from the Lord as a reward. It is the Lord Christ you are serving. (Col 3:22-24)

As we work, we're serving not just our bosses, not just the people who benefit from our work, but also the Lord Jesus (the one who tells us to love our neighbours). He promises a reward and, on his return, an inheritance for those who trust him.

If you're in a position of having people work for you, be careful about how you use that power, because the Boss of bosses is watching you. Consider this statement in Colossians: "Masters, provide your slaves with what is right and fair, because you know that you also have a Master in heaven" (Col 4:1). Bosses or supervisors—call them what you like—have a massive effect on the way their workers experience their jobs. The boss affects satisfaction, stress, even the psychological wellbeing of workers. A study by global consulting firm Korn Ferry notes that for many people their boss is the biggest source of stress at work:

> The survey shows 35% of the respondents say their boss is their biggest source of stress at work, and 80% say a change in leadership, such as a new direct manager or someone higher up the organizational chart, impacts their stress levels.[10]

10 Korn Ferry, *Workplace Stress Continues to Mount*, Korn Ferry website, 14 November 2018, accessed 7 January 2022 (kornferry.com/insights/articles/workplace-stress-motivation).

I can show you study after study, but if you've ever had a job and a boss, you already know that's true. So if you have people at work under your authority, you know what I'm going to say: man up and look after them.

There's one last thing to say about work to followers of Jesus: the workplace is where you'll know many people who aren't followers of Jesus and who may well have never seriously considered his teachings and claims. In fact, you may be the only Christian they will meet. Now, you're at work *to work* and to do your job properly. But it's also a great opportunity to talk with people at a personal level (when appropriate) about their spiritual beliefs, and to share your faith in Jesus as you have opportunity. Let's think about this in detail with three specific points:

a. People need to know you're a follower of Jesus

I know it can seem a little awkward being 'the religious one' in a group of people who clearly don't share your beliefs. In fact, sometimes when the topic of Jesus comes up people can react like they've opened the wrong door at Fukushima. But often that's not the case—in fact, you might be surprised. Even if it is the case, Jesus calls his followers to a public faith; to not be ashamed of him in front of other people: "If anyone is ashamed of me and my words in this adulterous and sinful generation, the Son of Man will be ashamed of them when he comes in his Father's glory with the holy angels" (Mark 8:38). So speak about your Christian life as opportunities come up naturally in conversation: "What did you do on the weekend? What do you think about this news story? What do you tell your kids about this issue?"

b. Be consistent in how you live

Our culture is moving even further away from its Christian roots at a rate of knots, but at a personal level people of faith will almost always be treated with respect if we're consistent in the way we live. People can smell hypocrisy a mile off. (Incidentally, the new term for hypocrisy seems to be 'virtue signalling'.) And they're watching you—especially once you've ticked off point (a) above and let them know you follow Jesus. If you are consistent in how you speak and act, it will give credibility to your words about Jesus.

c. Pray for opportunities to share your faith

When it comes to speaking about Jesus, you can't force-feed people. There are many stories of bad memories from religious schools where people felt religion was forced onto them. So we need to listen carefully to people about where they are 'spiritually' before we speak. But there *will* be opportunities to speak about our faith.

The apostle Paul asks the Christians in Colossae to pray that he will have opportunities: "And pray for us, too, that God may open a door for our message, so that we may proclaim the mystery of Christ, for which I am in chains" (Col 4:3). He also asks the Christians in Ephesus to pray that he would have courage to take those opportunities:

> Pray also for me, that whenever I speak, words may be given me so that I will fearlessly make known the mystery of the gospel, for which I am an ambassador in chains. Pray that I may declare it fearlessly, as I should. (Eph 6:19-20)

If even the great apostle Paul needed prayer—for opportunities to happen in the first place, and for boldness to take them—how much more do we need to pray? So pray for opportunities to share the gospel with people; pray because you care for them. They're not 'projects'; they're friends, workmates, relatives, real people we care about, and so we want to share the great news of Jesus with them.

My friend Peter, who is very gifted at speaking with people

about Jesus, works with City Bible Forum.[11] He has three key values in dealing with people who aren't yet followers of Jesus, and he keeps reminding his team and everyone else about these values: we must act with *humility*, *patience* and *respect*. It is God who changes hearts through the message of Jesus. Just as Paul prayed, we should ask God to give us the opportunities to speak and the courage to take them.

---

11 City Bible Forum is an Australian Christian organization aiming to share the message of Jesus in the workplace. They have great resources, both in training material to help Christians know how to explain the gospel, and also talks, seminars and articles (under the 'Third Space' logo) that can be shared with people to explain the gospel message; see citybibleforum.org and thirdspace.org.au. (Full disclosure: I've been involved with City Bible Forum for many years.) You could also search for other similar workplace ministries in your local area, or talk to your church pastor about getting some help and support.

10. MAN UP AS A SINGLE MAN

To be honest, me writing on 'singleness' is a bit like me writing on hair care, and I've been bald as a badger for 24 years.

Singleness? I was married at the age of 22. Our fortieth wedding anniversary is in the rear-vision mirror. So yes, I've been married forever. But I've had many, many conversations with single men who have been open with me about life. So I invite you to read these humble suggestions for single men and form your own conclusions (knowing, of course, that the real wisdom will be found in the Bible).

There's a bad smell around in our culture. It's the idea that living as a single man is second rate or incomplete—that it marks you out as a loser in the game of life.

It's a bad smell because it's a lie.

When asked the best and worst thing about being single today, a young Christian man told me:

> The best thing is not having to worry about someone else when making big decisions. The worst is realizing that may always be the case—that lack of complete intimacy with someone, potentially for always, can be very intimidating. Also, to be frank, a sexless life looks appalling if I let myself think about that.

There are many reasons why men are single, or unmarried, and there are a whole range of emotions that come with those reasons. Maybe you're single because you're young and haven't really thought about it much—you're not yet of marrying age. Or maybe you're older and have decided that marriage isn't for you. Or maybe you are older and would like to be married but the opportunity (aka: the right girl) hasn't presented itself (or herself) yet. Or you may be single because you're divorced or separated, or a widower—with all the heartache that those situations bring. Things are even harder if you have children and you don't have all the opportunity to be with them that you would like.

Let's look at some of the positives and the negatives of being single.

The positives of living as a single man

There are obviously lots of positives about the single life. A single man has a freedom that a man with a bunch of kids, a people mover and a cardigan just doesn't have. If you have little kids, there's a 45-minute departure routine just to leave the house during the day. And you're not going out anywhere at night, because your 8 kg human alarm clock is waking at 4:30 am regardless of what you do. The single man has freedoms that the family man doesn't have, not just in the hours he keeps but also in where he chooses to live—and not just the size of the house or unit, but the neighbourhood, city, and even the country he chooses to live in. The single man travels lighter, cheaper and faster.

There are also the financial obligations single men don't carry. If you've not been married before and have no children, you're probably only responsible for feeding one mouth. This will give you the ability to be generous financially. Seriously, money is power—the power to help look after other people or support the right causes. The great temptation for single men is to live selfishly, 'just for me'. But singleness gives the freedom and resources to man up and care for other people.

For the man who follows Jesus, the single life gives great opportunity in how you use this freedom. The apostle Paul says in 1 Corinthians 7:

> I would like you to be free from concern. An unmarried man is concerned about the Lord's affairs—how he can please the Lord. But a married man is concerned about the affairs of this world—how he can please his wife—and his interests are divided. (1 Cor 7:32-34a)

Regarding marriage or singleness, Paul isn't saying one way is right and another way is wrong. It's simply that marriage and family bring responsibilities and obligations that a single man doesn't have, and singleness brings a different set of freedoms and opportunities.

Timothy and Kathy Keller explain what Paul means by the 'gift' of singleness in their book *The Meaning of Marriage*:

> In his writings, Paul always uses the word 'gift' to mean an ability God gives to build others up. Paul is not speaking, then, of some kind of elusive, stress-free state. The 'gift-ness' of being single for Paul lay in the freedom it gave him to concentrate on ministry in ways that a married man could not. Paul may very well, then, have experienced what we today would call an 'emotional struggle' with singleness. He might have wanted to be married. He not only found an ability to live a life of service to God and others in that situation, he discovered (and capitalized on) the unique features of single life (such as time flexibility) to minister with very great effectiveness.[1]

---

1   T Keller and K Keller, *The Meaning of Marriage: Facing the complexities of commitment with the wisdom of God*, Hodder and Stoughton, 2011, pp 207-208.

So there's a challenge if you're single. How are you using that extra freedom you have? How can you get on the front foot with those opportunities? Whose lives will you invest in, with your time and energy and finances? If you're a follower of Jesus, what priorities has he given you to be, as Paul said above, "concerned about the Lord's affairs"?

The negatives of living as a single man

But there are also many ways in which it's not easy to live as a single man. Loneliness can be a big one. Yes, there's freedom to live wherever you want, go on holidays wherever you want. But what about the flip side: who do you live with? Who do you go on holidays with?

This obviously highlights the importance of long-term friendships with other blokes, but also with couples and whole families. To be close with families, friends and hopefully with your own extended family can be fun and fulfilling. Think about being an uncle who turns up to enjoy time with nieces and nephews—whether biological, or through friendship with the parents of their 'honorary' nieces and nephews. In chapter 8, I spent some time dealing with the issue of loneliness, and much of that applies to the potential loneliness of singleness.

One of the best answers to loneliness is to belong to a community of people who care for one another. Jesus' plan for this is called a *church*. For the man who follows Jesus, there's a bigger welcoming family structure, and God deliberately designed it to meet many of our social, relational needs. To put that into simple words: if you follow Jesus, get yourself involved in a church—a church community that takes the Bible seriously. If they do that, they'll love Jesus, love one another, and welcome you.

Of course, the elephant in the room for single men is sex—or, more accurately, the lack of it, if you follow Jesus' teaching on the matter. If you're not a follower of Jesus, the issue may not seem as obvious, but Jesus' call for the Christian is to live a life that is radically different from the world around him, particularly in the area of sexuality. This isn't because Jesus is the fun police; it's for our good.[2]

Why does the Bible tell us not to have sex outside of a committed, lifelong, faithful, publicly recognized, heterosexual relationship (i.e. marriage)? Let me give some of the main strands of thought or reasons that our Creator insists (and commands) this is his way to live and the best way to live.

The Bible is very positive about sex; it says that we should enjoy sex within marriage. The Song of Songs in the Old Testament is a long, poetic celebration of erotic love within marriage. In 1 Corinthians, the apostle Paul says husbands and wives should meet each other's sexual needs. It's a command:

> But since sexual immorality is occurring, each man should have sexual relations with his own wife, and each woman with her own husband. The husband should fulfil his marital duty to his wife, and likewise the wife to her husband. The wife does not have authority over her own body but yields it to her husband. In the same way, the husband does not have authority over his own body but yields it to his wife. Do not deprive each other except perhaps by mutual

---

2   In this book, I've said that the Bible defines marriage as being between one man and one woman. This raises an obvious question: What about those of us who are same-sex attracted? This is a very real struggle for lots of men and a really important topic, but a full discussion is beyond the scope of what I want to cover here. For those wanting to think more about this issue, I'd recommend: C Keane (ed), *What Some of You Were*, Matthias Media, 2001; V Roberts, *Battles Christians Face*, Authentic Media, 2007 (especially chapter 7); S Allberry, *Is God Anti-Gay?*, The Good Book Company, 2013; and the website for Living Faith, a Sydney ministry that encourages Christian faithfulness in sexuality (livingfaith.online). It can also be very wise to seek support from a trusted Christian friend or the pastor of your local church.

consent and for a time, so that you may devote yourselves to prayer. Then come together again so that Satan will not tempt you because of your lack of self-control. (1 Cor 7:2-5)

Sex is not just for the creation of babies, but for bonding and intimacy and, well, for having great fun. The Bible speaks of couples becoming 'one flesh' in the act of sexual intimacy (Gen 2:24; Matt 19:6; 1 Cor 6:16). Sexual intercourse or the sexual relationship is not just a physical act; there's also a personal, even spiritual side to it. Physically, when you have sex with someone, you bond with them in a special way. Oxytocin—sometimes known as the 'love hormone'—is released in both men and women to produce this emotional bonding.[3]

A sexual relationship is meant to be a huge part of the 'glue' that bonds a man and woman together for life. That's why sex is to be reserved for that special, lifelong relationship. Timothy and Kathy Keller explain it like this:

If sex is a method that God invented to do 'whole life entrustment' and self-giving, it should not surprise us that sex makes us feel deeply connected to the other person even when used wrongly. Unless you deliberately disable it or through practice you numb the original impulse, sex makes you feel personally interwoven and joined to another human being as you are literally physically joined. ... Therefore, if you have sex outside marriage, you will have to steel yourself against sex's power to soften your heart towards another person and make you more trusting. The problem is that eventually sex will lose its covenant-making power for you even if you one day get married. Ironically, then, sex

3   For a brief article on oxytocin, see M MacGill, 'What is the link between love and oxytocin?', *Medical News Today*, 4 September 2017, accessed 7 January 2022 (medicalnewstoday.com/articles/275795.php).

outside of marriage eventually works backwards, making you less able to commit and trust another person.[4]

The sexual relationship was created to be the most profound and intimate of all relationships, and so when this is misused and abused we have the ability to hurt each other most profoundly.

As a society, we are now beginning to understand the extremely serious nature of sexual abuse. It deeply damages people, which is most obvious and most tragic when children or young people are involved. But adults can also be profoundly wounded. Sexual abuse damages a person mentally, emotionally and spiritually. It needs to be taken with the utmost seriousness, both in protecting the vulnerable and in dealing with perpetrators.

Even when sex involves two consenting adults, people can hurt each other; something that should be about building lifelong intimacy is so often treated casually or selfishly. That's why the apostle Paul says we should run from sexual sin: it actually involves our bodies, our very selves: "Flee from sexual immorality. All other sins a person commits are outside the body, but whoever sins sexually, sins against their own body" (1 Cor 6:18).

The good news is that God offers forgiveness and cleansing and restoration, regardless of what we've done. God is ready to forgive us because Jesus died to take the penalty we deserve, to pay the price of forgiveness.[5] (I'll say much more about this in the conclusion, about following the greatest man.) But to be forgiven means then turning away from the wrong we've done. The Bible's word for that is 'repentance': turning away from sin and turning to Jesus in trust. With regard to sexuality, that will mean trusting God in how we live, trusting that he cares for us and he does know what is best.

---

4   Keller and Keller, *The Meaning of Marriage*, pp 226-227.
5   Remember 1 Corinthians 6:9-11, the wonderful passage on forgiveness and a fresh start that we saw back in chapter 5.

I know this is a tough call. For many men who are Christian, this is the sharp edge of living out our trust in Jesus. Or to use another cliché, it really is where the rubber hits the road. Will you trust him in this area?[6]

One of the things that can make it hard to be single is the belief that "If I were just married, all my problems would be solved". That pretty obviously isn't the case. I've known plenty of men who have been in difficult marriages, and they stay because they have made promises and they want to look after their children. Believe me, there are plenty of married men who think, "If I were just single, all my problems would be solved". It's also worth noting that in our hedonistic society the quest to be *happy* is so often the goal in life. But pursuit of happiness is like dedicating your life to grasping fog: hard to get hold of, and even harder to hold on to.

The Bible doesn't tell us to pursue happiness; happiness is great, but it's an emotion that comes and goes depending on circumstances. Instead, we are told to value and learn the secret of *contentment*. The apostle Paul speaks of learning contentment, and the great difference it made to his life:

> I have learned to be content whatever the circumstances. I know what it is to be in need, and I know what it is to have plenty. I have learned the secret of being content in any and every situation, whether well fed or hungry, whether living in plenty or in want. I can do all this through him who gives me strength. (Phil 4:11-13)

The last verse of this passage seems to be a favourite of Christian athletes. But notice that Paul is not saying Jesus will give his people power to win in all situations; he's saying that Jesus will

---

6   For further reading on this topic, I recommend PD Jensen and T Payne, *Pure Sex*, Matthias Media, 2003; and Keller and Keller, *The Meaning of Marriage*.

give his people the strength to be *content* even in the face of hardship and suffering. Put simply, the key to contentment is being able to appreciate and enjoy the good things God gives us; to enjoy those good things in the present and be thankful to God: "The fear of the Lord leads to life; then one rests content, untouched by trouble" (Prov 19:23).

If you want to get married

If you're single but you do want to get married, you should read the chapter in this book on being a husband. To follow Jesus and be the sort of husband he wants you to be is a very serious commitment. If, after reading that, you're still keen to take on the responsibility, here are some thoughts on what's important to consider.

a. Get your life in order

I know it's not simple, and there are different issues at different stages of life, but this is the place to start. Become the kind of man that the right woman wants to commit to. Sure, there's no 'one size fits all' for what a woman wants, but we can be pretty certain of some common things. In my own stumbling way, I've written this whole book about becoming that kind of man.

Women want men, not boys. If you're not sure of the difference, re-read chapter 4 ('Initiation: From boys to men'). Here's Jordan Peterson's take on this:

> If they're healthy, women don't want boys. They want men. They want someone to contend with; someone to grapple with. If they're tough, they want someone tougher. If they're smart, they want someone smarter. They desire someone who brings to the table something they can't already provide. This often makes it hard for tough, smart,

attractive women to find mates: there just aren't that many men around who can outclass them enough to be considered desirable (who are higher, as one research publication put it, in "income, education, self-confidence, intelligence, dominance and social position").[7]

I don't agree with everything Dr Peterson says in the quote above. In particular, I think he's wrong about a woman wanting a man who's tougher and smarter and who can "outclass" her. But I guarantee this: a woman wants a man, not a boy. She wants a grown-up. She wants someone who she can rely on. She wants a man who fits our definition of healthy masculinity: *a willingness to take responsibility and use the power you have to care for and nurture those around you.*

It's also worth saying that when you're looking for a partner, you may well find a woman who is smarter or more capable than you in some areas. I found exactly that in my wife. Kathy is a genius with money, administration, organization and—best of all—cooking. She also has this Jedi intuition about people and their characters. So what should I do? It's obvious: let her be good at what she's good at (she manages our finances, runs our household admin, and loves to cook—it's a beautiful thing). I should encourage her to use her gifts and be glad that she has them. The great challenge (with the big reward) is to work out how you complement each other's abilities as a couple.

A woman wants a man; that is, she wants a man she can trust and rely on. Learn some of this book's hard lessons about being responsible and reliable, about having the power to keep on turning up at things that matter, about learning the humility of the five hard truths mentioned in chapter 4. Financial stability is a big plus, too.

---

7   Peterson, *12 Rules for Life,* p 209.

Of course, if you are a Christian, working on what the Bible calls 'godliness' is the most important thing. To work and pray at becoming more like Jesus in how you treat people (for example, learning to be both strong and compassionate) and in your values and life goals is the greatest priority—not just because it will make you more attractive as a potential husband, but because it is honouring to your Lord, Jesus.

Does getting your life in order guarantee that you'll find the right girl and live happily ever after? Obviously not. But even if it doesn't happen as you want, everything mentioned above will still make your life better and will make you a greater blessing to the people around you, whether or not one of those people ends up becoming your wife.

b. Understand what's truly valuable

If you're a follower of Jesus, don't get emotionally or romantically involved with a woman who doesn't share your faith. The Bible is clear on this. If the believer has a choice about who to marry, it must be another follower of Jesus:

> A woman is bound to her husband as long as he lives. But if her husband dies, she is free to marry anyone she wishes, but he must belong to the Lord. (1 Cor 7:39)[8]

In context, this is describing a woman who has a choice of marriage partner, but the principle obviously applies to any Christian choosing a marriage partner: you must choose another Christian to marry.

There are good reasons for this. The Christian man says following Jesus is the most important thing in his life. If you start a relationship with a woman, it will end in one of only two ways:

---

8   See also 2 Corinthians 6:14, which stresses not being bound tightly with those who are not believers. In context, this verse is about false teachers in the Corinthian church, but this also has great relevance to marriage.

you'll break up, or you'll get married. It is really dumb to plan to become one—emotionally, physically and spiritually—with someone who doesn't share your faith. It will mean you cannot share the central thing in your life (faith in Jesus) with your wife. How will your children be brought up? Will your wife agree to financially supporting Christian ministry? Will she agree to you spending time at church and in other Christian activities? Being married to a woman who isn't a follower of Jesus will be very difficult and a pressure on your own personal faith, rather than a support and encouragement in it.[9]

I know Christian men who are married to non-Christian women. The men I'm thinking of do a good job of loving and caring for their wives, but it's not easy, and their greatest desire is for their wives to come to faith in Jesus. If you are going out with a woman who's not a believer and you have no intention of ever marrying her—if you regard that as not even a possibility—then you are just using her. Seriously. Will you get to a certain point in the relationship and then just tell her she's 'terminated'? If you don't intend the relationship to progress to a lifelong commitment, man up and end the relationship as gently as possible, so she can meet someone who will be willing to commit to her.

Timothy and Kathy Keller explain the need to marry within your faith like this:

> Many think it is very narrow-minded indeed to discourage Christians from marrying outside of their faith, but there are strong reasons for this biblical rule. If your partner doesn't share your Christian faith, then he or she doesn't truly understand it as you do, from the inside. And if Jesus

---

9   Of course, if you are already married to a woman who isn't a believer (e.g. if you've become a Christian after you were married, but she hasn't), you should love her and stay with her. See 1 Corinthians 7:12: "If any brother has a wife who is not a believer and she is willing to live with him, he must not divorce her."

is central to you, then that means that your partner doesn't truly understand you. He or she doesn't understand the mainspring of your life, the ground motive of all you do. ... The essence of intimacy in marriage is that finally you have someone who will eventually come to understand you and accept you as you are. Your spouse should be someone you don't have to hide from or always be 'spinning'; it should be someone who 'gets' you. But if the person is not a believer, he or she can't understand your very essence and heart.[10]

Once you've resolved that you'll only consider marrying someone who "belong[s] to the Lord", it's worth thinking in more detail about what you are looking for in a wife. Good looks are great, and you need to find her attractive—I don't really need to say that. But given that marriage is a lifelong relationship, you need to focus on things that won't be affected by time and gravity. Over years and years, so many things wrinkle, sag and fade—for her and for you—but character, heart and values aren't affected by time and gravity. I guess I've just said in a crass and clumsy way what the apostle Peter says in a beautiful way when he describes a woman who walks with Jesus. Peter says that a woman's beauty should be that of her "inner self, the unfading beauty of a gentle and quiet spirit, which is of great worth in God's sight" (1 Pet 3:4).

If you're a man who follows Jesus, you want to find a woman who cares a lot for you, but who cares more for Jesus than for you. This is really the secret to finding the right woman. In Christian or biblical terms, you're looking for a godly woman, and if she is a godly woman, she's going to be looking for a man who clearly follows Jesus.

There are other considerations, too. Put simply, is the 'spark' there? In other words, do you want to wake up beside this

10 Keller and Keller, *The Meaning of Marriage*, pp 209-210.

woman every morning for the rest of your life? But a much better question to ask would be "Am I prepared to lay down my life day by day to love and care for this woman?" After all, that's what God calls you to do as a husband.

c. When you meet her

Don't die wondering. Ask her out. I'm a little out of practice with dating; the last time I asked a girl out was in 1979. But I do know one thing for sure: you'll never know if you never have a go.

If you start dating (for want of a better word), what are you doing other than going to a new movie or eating at a restaurant with actual tablecloths? It's really all about working out how you relate as a couple. Does it work for you to take the initiative to care for her? What's her response to that? Is it natural for you both? Can you see that working out long-term? (For more on what I have in mind here, see chapter 11: 'Man up as a husband'.)

One last thing—before you're married, keep your hands off her. That's right, you read that correctly. The Bible says the only place for sexual intimacy is inside marriage—between a man and a woman who are already in that lifelong, committed, faithful, publicly recognized relationship. So, if you're going out with a lady, keep your hands off her. You know what I mean.

Okay, let me spell it out: don't sexually arouse one another.

Why? Because it's not best for her, and it's not best for you. And you know that.

Take a step back and imagine something with me. The woman you're going to marry is out there somewhere. She may even be going out with some random bloke. How do you want Mr Random to treat your bride-to-be? With absolute purity, of course (cf. 1 Tim 5:2), because you know that will be absolutely best for her and for you. And that is exactly the way you should treat any woman *you* go out with. Treat her the way you want Mr Random to treat the woman you're going to marry. Treat her with purity, absolutely, because she will be someone's bride one day. Maybe yours; maybe not.

I know that's not easy, but God says this for a reason. Bonding as a couple at a physical level happens very quickly. As soon as sexual intimacy happens, all sorts of hormones start pumping. God has wired us up with all sorts of good stuff like that to help us bond for life. In the right context (i.e. marriage), sex is a great thing. It's the glue that helps marriages stay together. It's also lots of fun. But all those hormones are powerful. They temporarily stop you thinking—at least with your brain.

Some people refer to this state of mind as 'limerence', a feeling of intense infatuation. In the country town where I grew up, less refined labels were used. Once you get sexually involved with someone, you can't make clear decisions about the other person and whether they could (or should) be your life partner. The question is not "Am I attracted to her?" or "Is she physically beautiful?" but "Can I, will I, devote my life to caring for this woman?"

Limerence wears off after 18 months to three years, so if that was the basis of the relationship you're in deep trouble as a couple. The other reason to keep your hands off her—and I'm speaking particularly to you if you're a Christian man—is that taking the lead and treating the woman you're going out with in this way (i.e. with purity and respect) means she will grow in her respect for you and your capacity to take the lead and honour and care for her. As a potential husband, that's exactly how you should treat her. And that's how you want her, your potential wife, to feel about you. I know it's not easy. I know it takes massive amounts of self-control. But it will be worth it. Whatever God says in this regard is for our benefit.

When, as a new believer, I started going out with the great girl who is now my wife, I didn't get this right. I should have been more self-controlled with her, and I should have treated her with more honour and love. If I had that time over again, I'd do it differently.

So, to pull some threads together: the single life is in no way inferior to the married life; there are different challenges, and there are different benefits. For the man who follows Jesus, it should be pretty obvious that to be single isn't deficient in any way, as Jesus himself never married. The apostle Paul lived as a single man for decades. The challenge in any man's life is to learn contentment—to appreciate the good things in his life, and to deal with the hardships in the strength that Jesus provides—and to man up by using his power to care for others. Singleness can be God's way of opening up a whole range of opportunities for you to do just that.

Living as a single man

By J

Trying to distil 38 years of living as a single Christian man is a difficult thing to do. The experience of being single—or at least unmarried—will vary for everyone. I am not someone who has 'the gift of singleness'. I have never felt that God has called me to a single life, and I never desired to remain unmarried. But I have, at times, come to view singleness as a gift. With that introduction, I will try to impart some of what I have learned along the way.

1. Identity and security

First and foremost, I have come to understand that struggling with singleness is really another variation on what we all struggle with as humans. The question that underpins the struggle is: Where do we find our identity and security?

Walking closely with married couples that then have children, my observation is that they are often distracted from this struggle by a partner or their families. They get security from their partner and purpose from being a parent, and they often just lack time to even stop and think. When things get hard, though, they struggle with the same existential questions. Ultimately, if they are not grounded in their faith and working on their relationship with God then their families offer a false sense of security.

As I have focused on developing my relationship with and dependence on God, the need for a partner as security has diminished. Learning that my significance comes from being God's son, much loved and sought after, despite many attempts on my part to leave, has also assisted me in ceasing to seek out physical connections to fill the gaps and hide from feeling alone. This has meant at times crying out to God in anguish or anger, questioning why he has not provided a partner (or the right job, or enough friends, or any number of other things). Honesty with God has been an important part of my reliance on and trust in him.

2. Temptation and honesty

Over the years, I've dated some great women for maybe an average of four months at a time, never more than 12 months. Despite my faith and a desire to adhere to God's call to wait until marriage for sex, there have also been instances of 'dates' that were never intended to extend beyond the one encounter. I kept these separate from my relationships and dated Christian women with whom I had godly boundaries. It wasn't healthy, but it was the reality of my struggle, and I do not doubt it's the same for others.

If you are struggling with temptation, pornography, sex, or whatever, don't struggle alone. For a long time, I carried a huge amount of shame about having a sex life. As the son of a pastor trying to appear like a good Christian, serving in the church, I thought I couldn't possibly talk about it. There was also a fair dose of pride in there. Once I did open up to some people, I found the space to step back from trying to appear like a good Christian. I ceased serving in ways I was not morally qualified to be undertaking in a church, sought accountability, and worked hard to develop a healthy and abstinent approach to sex.

3. Investing in relationships

You don't have to be single alone. A lot of single people I know have felt left behind as they have grown older. However, I was 'blessed' with the bad example of two long-term single family members. I observed them pushing away their married siblings and at times resenting my siblings and me (especially when we got in the way as children). So I always made a point of investing in relationships.

If my single friends were no longer single, I would become their girlfriend or boyfriend's friend. I would invest in their relationship as a couple. I've never been afraid of being a third wheel—or a fifth wheel, or a seventh. As a result, over the years I have been blessed with being able to sow into people's marriages and to observe in sometimes intimate ways things I otherwise would not have seen. I've also developed great friendships with a lot of guys because I was conscious of my need for single and available friends, and so have sought them out.

I also spend quality time with each of my nieces and nephews. I'm an awesome uncle. Being like this was not always easy and has come with its fair share of feeling slighted or let down. I understand the desire to stop trying.

But you can't complain about feeling lonely if you are not taking the time to invest or pressing on through the disappointments.

4. Have good, close friendships with people of the opposite sex

This can be hard in a church context, and is actually discouraged in some churches. But I have benefited hugely in being able to have real conversations with women without other guys around. When there is openness and no romantic pressure, you really can learn a lot about each other.

Obviously, being clear about your intentions and seeking to understand theirs is pretty important here. If you are being friends with someone because you are seeking a relationship, be up front. Developing a friendship is a great basis for a relationship *if* that is what you're both doing. Conversely, if you do not have a romantic interest, don't enjoy the company of a woman who might be keen on you because it boosts your ego. Figure the situation out and seek to protect her heart.

This brings me to my last point.

5. Patience

God knows his timing, and we do not. I now assume that I will most likely remain unmarried, and I have no doubt that it will always be a grief and a struggle. I still ask God for a wife, but I have reached a point where I am determined to live a life that is full and glorifying to him despite being single. I have largely let go of resenting singleness and I can now see how good it can be. I can genuinely say that I am ready and willing to be alone. I also do not believe that God will provide a partner for everyone.

I share this with you as an honest account. Our hope is

in God alone. If he has started a good work in you, then he will complete it. If we continue to put our trust in him, then we will learn more and more deeply that he will work in all things for the good of those who love and follow him.

11. MAN UP AS A HUSBAND

H ERE'S THE SECRET to being a good husband in three words: *don't be selfish*. There it is. Pure and simple. In fact, it's the secret to pretty much any relationship. If it's true of every relationship, it's especially true of the most intimate of all human relationships.

It may be very simple, but it's not easy. That is, we're naturally selfish. Selfishness is the default setting of the human heart. If you're a follower of Jesus, you will probably have understood this. For some of us who haven't read what Jesus taught about this, it might be a new idea.[1]

When it comes to marriage, selfishness doesn't just creep in over years; it can set up home right from the beginning. And I believe men especially have that natural inclination to selfishness. I know—I am one. If you're married, it's quite possible that when you first met the lady you're married to, you fell in love not so much with her but with how she made you feel. Romantic love (let's call it that for the moment) is really about 'how you make me feel'. Almost every love song ever written is about that. Romantic love as I've defined it here is a kind of love, but you can't build a marriage on it because it doesn't last. The bath water inevitably cools down.

Marriage is a great opportunity for selfishness. In fact, if you

---

1 See Mark 7:20-23. For further background, see Genesis 3.

want to be confronted with the reality of your own selfishness in all its ugliness, probably the best strategy is to get married. When you're thrown together with another person for life, there's nowhere for your selfishness to hide. To make a marriage really work requires deliberate effort and a different understanding of love. It means learning to love in the way that God wants us to.

In this chapter, let's look firstly at how our society's understanding of marriage is being changed or warped by selfishness and at the pressure this is putting on marriage relationships in two different directions. Secondly, we'll look at the brand of selfishness that's a particular problem for men, and why we need to man up as husbands.

Marriage and the big 'ME'

Much of the problem with marriages has come from a change in the understanding of what marriage is actually about and what people are doing when they get married. I'm sure Timothy and Kathy Keller are right as they talk about the way in which an understanding of marriage has changed over the years, from a contract between a man and a woman to raise a family in a stable environment, to today's expectation that marriage should be about personal fulfilment: "Marriage used to be about us, but now it's about me."[2]

The ultimate example of this has to be 'sologamy', the word used to describe people who marry themselves. It's a growing phenomenon—wedding ceremony, wedding dress, wedding cake, the works.[3] Seriously, you couldn't make this stuff up. It really is 'all about me' taken to the extreme. Critics claim it's just a tad

2   Keller and Keller, *The Meaning of Marriage*, p 29.
3   D Tali, 'Why growing numbers are saying "yes" to themselves', *BBC News Business*, 22 December 2017, accessed 7 January 2022 (bbc.com/news/business-42415394).

narcissistic. Seems a reasonable criticism. I guess an obvious upside is you know who you're getting as in-laws; no surprises there. But the downside would be if it doesn't work out, the divorce is going to be really awkward.

Meanwhile, back on planet earth, two significant trends are unfolding. First, many people are devaluing marriage by just 'shacking up'. "We don't need a piece of paper!" they say. "We'll stay together as long as we feel like it." This really is selfishness showing itself as a reluctance to commit—because, after all, something or someone better might come along.

But another trend is taking hold at the same time: people are investing so much in marriage that the relationship is being crushed under unrealistic expectations. As Timothy and Kathy Keller explain, "modern people make the painfulness of marriage even greater than it has to be, because they crush it under the weight of their almost cosmically impossible expectations".[4] Once a person starts looking to marriage and their partner to be "the meaning of life" for them—to be the thing they worship—they are bound to be let down. The only one who can carry the weight of being god in our lives is God himself.

So on one hand our society devalues marriage, making it optional or a matter of convenience, while on the other hand we look for it to be the ultimate fairytale that will give us the meaning of life. That's why the expectations around weddings keep on creeping up. The average wedding in Australia now costs the equivalent of the GDP of a small country in the developing world.[5] There's a whole industry that will 'help' couples spend an arm and a leg on the fairytale day that's supposed to ensure that they live happily ever after—well, at least ensure that they look

4 Keller and Keller, *The Meaning of Marriage*, p 41.
5 A Duncan, 'How much does an average wedding cost in Australia?', *Canstar*, 17 September 2021, accessed 7 January 2022 (canstar.com.au/budgeting/what-does-a-wedding-cost).

good on Instagram and Facebook.

In the real world, of course, marriage will be hard work—maybe not all the time, and not all in the same way, but all marriages will be difficult at some time. There are some obvious reasons why, such as the simple fact that it takes a long time to get to know someone. The Kellers say:

> When you first fall in love, you think you love the person, but you don't really. You can't know who the person is right away. That takes years. You actually love your idea of the person—and that is always, at first, one dimensional and somewhat mistaken.[6]

As I said above, romantic love is really about how *you* make *me* feel. It's good fun, but it fades. Even in the best of relationships, the bubble bath of romantic love cools, and you're left with the bath water of reality. It takes work to keep that bath water warm. The good news is that if you're working at it, you can keep the water warm—and you can still make some bubbles too, just not all the time. I'll share a few thoughts on keeping things warm later in this chapter.

I know I'll get into real trouble for this, but here goes: the expectations about marriage and relationships, around personal fulfilment, and especially around fairytale weddings seem to be more of an issue for women than for men. But it's in the area of selfishness that men excel. It's not subtle; it's just plain old selfishness. And as is so often the case, it's made worse by something good being twisted and used wrongly. That 'something' is the good, biblical idea of male 'headship' within marriage.

6 Keller and Keller, *The Meaning of Marriage,* p 94.

Marriage, men and 'headship'

Selfishness is an even more pointed issue for men in marriage because of the responsibility we are given and the temptation to use it in the wrong way. I'm talking about headship and submission in marriage.

Generally today, if you're feeling masochistic, you could put two or three cats in a bag, shake it, and stick your head in the bag. Or if you can't find any cats, just start a conversation in a mixed audience about headship and submission in marriage. This is a teaching that's misunderstood by a world that doesn't follow Jesus. Sometimes, it's misapplied and abused by those who claim to follow Jesus. There are volumes written on this subject; some are useful, while many are not.[7] If you are a follower of Jesus and a husband, you need to take this biblical teaching very seriously for at least two reasons. Firstly, God will hold you accountable for how you care for your wife. It matters very much how you treat her. Secondly, you can be sure this is the best way to live, the best way to behave in your marriage, because all God's commandments are for our good. He created us. He created marriage. He knows what's best. To do your job as a husband you will need to man up—but you need to do it Jesus' way, not the world's way. If you're not yet Jesus' man, read on carefully as we look at what Jesus calls his men to do as husbands. It's not easy, but it's good— very good.

Here's the key New Testament passage on marriage. It's found in the book of Ephesians:

> [21] Submit to one another out of reverence for Christ.
> [22] Wives, submit yourselves to your own husbands as you do to the Lord. [23] For the husband is the head of the wife as

---

7   See a list of recommended books on a Christian view of marriage at the end of this chapter.

Christ is the head of the church, his body, of which he is the Saviour. [24] Now as the church submits to Christ, so also wives should submit to their husbands in everything.

[25] Husbands, love your wives, just as Christ loved the church and gave himself up for her [26] to make her holy, cleansing her by the washing with water through the word, [27] and to present her to himself as a radiant church, without stain or wrinkle or any other blemish, but holy and blameless. [28] In this same way, husbands ought to love their wives as their own bodies. He who loves his wife loves himself. [29] After all, no-one ever hated their own body, but they feed and care for their body, just as Christ does the church— [30] for we are members of his body. [31] "For this reason a man will leave his father and mother and be united to his wife, and the two will become one flesh." [32] This is a profound mystery— but I am talking about Christ and the church. [33] However, each one of you also must love his wife as he loves himself, and the wife must respect her husband. (Eph 5:21-33)

The husband is the head of the marriage. Yep, yahoo! But before you throw your hat in the air and grab the remote control to settle onto the couch, keep reading. We need to be very clear on what headship *is* and *is not*.

Yes, headship (as outlined in verses 23-26 in the passage above) is about authority, and it's modelled on Jesus' own authority as head of the church (his people gathered into a community). But it's an authority based on sacrificial love—*just as Christ loved the church and gave himself up for her*.

In the book *Recovering Biblical Manhood and Womanhood*, George Knight explains:

First, the loving husband gives of himself. In this leadership role as head, he seeks to lead by giving of himself to his wife in ways analogous to how Christ gave Himself to His bride.

Christ's giving of Himself was personal and sacrificial. This great principle of self-giving sets the tone and points toward the many ways in which this love can be manifested and realized.[8]

We could use the word 'lead' as in the above quote, but it seems better to say "take the initiative in caring for her" or perhaps best of all "show practical love for her". The great reality that the apostle Paul says husbands should copy is to love her the way Jesus loved his church, his people: he gave his life for her (them).

If you're a husband and you've chosen to follow Jesus, you've also signed up to love your wife in this way. This laying down of life will probably not happen in one big event, although sometimes it does. It's interesting how often witnesses to mass shootings report that men instinctively shield their wives or girlfriends with their own bodies. Put like that, most husbands would like to think, "Yes, I'd take a bullet for her". Quick, spontaneous, heroic—and almost inevitably a fantasy. Reality? You'd take a bullet for her, great, but will you do the dishes for her? Or visit your mother-in-law with her? And I mean *happily* visit her mum. That's much tougher. It's not quick, spontaneous or a fantasy. It's real. But you know what? In its own way, it's heroic. Married life is a thousand small decisions to put her first—to take the initiative to do what is best for her. Or, to put it in really simple, mundane terms, to be unselfish.

What's her part in this? See verse 22 in the passage above: "Wives, submit yourselves to your own husbands as you do to the Lord". The word 'submit' in the original language means 'to rank yourself under someone'.[9] In context, this means a willing

---

8   GW Knight III, 'Husbands and wives as analogues of Christ and the church (Ephesians 5:21-33 and Colossians 3:18-19)', in J Piper and W Grudem (eds), *Recovering Biblical Manhood and Womanhood*, Crossway, 2006, p 172.

9   The Greek word is *hypotassō*.

response to a husband's sacrificial, loving leadership. Or to put it another way, the wife is called on to make it easy for her husband to sacrificially love her.

There are a few key things to notice here. For starters, read Ephesians 5 very carefully and you'll see that Paul doesn't tell men, "Be the head of the marriage"; he mentions that in the section to wives in verses 22-24. Rather, he commands husbands *twice* to love their wives: "husbands, love your wives" (v. 25); "husbands ought to love their wives as their own bodies" (v. 28).[10]

Regarding the instruction to submit, nowhere is the husband told to *make* his wife submit, nor is he permitted to make her submit. Got that? It's between your wife and God. Submission to her husband's loving leadership is her response to God's word to her, and she is to choose to do it. That's what God asks her to do as a follower of Jesus. She's told to respond so that it's easy for him to love her sacrificially. That does make her vulnerable if he isn't loving her that way.

By the way, in Ephesians 6 children are told to "obey" their parents. But wives are told to "submit". That is, she chooses to do this as an adult with the same rights, and with as much intelligence and experience, as her husband. She's not like one of the kids. She's an adult. The husband's sacrificial love for her doesn't depend on her submission. He is to love her anyway.

Are you starting to see why it's a big call to man up as a husband?

Let's drill down a bit further by taking out the words to wives and looking just at the words to husbands:

Submit to one another out of reverence for Christ. ...

Husbands, love your wives, just as Christ loved the church and gave himself up for her to make her holy, cleansing her by the washing with water through the word,

10 See Knight, 'Husbands and wives', p 171.

and to present her to himself as a radiant church, without stain or wrinkle or any other blemish, but holy and blameless. In this same way, husbands ought to love their wives as their own bodies. He who loves his wife loves himself. After all, no-one ever hated their own body, but they feed and care for their body, just as Christ does the church—for we are members of his body. "For this reason a man will leave his father and mother and be united to his wife, and the two will become one flesh." This is a profound mystery—but I am talking about Christ and the church. However, each one of you also must love his wife as he loves himself ...

The husband—as head of the marriage or family—is told to lay down his life for his wife in the way Jesus loved his church and gave his life for her. So, what does this love look like? After all, how can you control 'love'? You can't command an emotion, can you? That's certainly how our culture thinks. But the New Testament says something radically different. It says love can be commanded because love is, at least to some extent, independent of emotions. It all depends how you define love. Timothy and Kathy Keller say:

> Emotions can't be commanded, only actions, and so it is actions that Paul is demanding [in Ephesians 5]. He doesn't care how [husbands] feel on a given day or at a given moment—they must love their wives.[11]

CS Lewis points out that love as an emotion follows action. The commitment to love and the loving actions very often precede and are the beginning of the loving feelings that flow:

> The rule for all of us is perfectly simple. Do not waste time bothering whether you "love" your neighbour; act as if you

---

11 Keller and Keller, *The Meaning of Marriage*, p 103.

did. As soon as we do this we find one of the great secrets. When you are behaving as if you loved someone, you will presently come to love him. If you injure someone you dislike, you will find yourself disliking him more. If you do him a good turn, you will find yourself disliking him less.[12]

It's not that complicated. A husband is to love his wife in real, practical ways, day by day, every day. Feelings may come and go. But you're told to love your wife; that's what you've promised to do, so that's what you know you should do. But don't worry—as you do that every day, the loving feelings will get even stronger.

a. Headship does *not* mean abusing power

There is never any excuse to be rough, pushy or abusive with your wife. Never any excuse to bully or intimidate her. Never any excuse to be controlling or manipulative.

Never.

I trust you've understood the point I'm trying to make.

In fact, a Christian wife is not called on to submit to, or to accept, abusive behaviour. She's called on to submit or respond willingly to love from her husband. There may be room for full and frank discussions between adults, sure, but a husband must *never* use his greater size or strength, his louder voice, his financial power—or whatever he may have—to intimidate her or abuse her or manipulate her. His role is the exact opposite. All these strengths are to be used to love and care for his wife. I'm not saying a husband allows himself to be browbeaten or under her thumb, but you know what I mean. The husband is to take the initiative in loving and looking after her.

No abusive behaviour, ever. Period.

---

12 Lewis, *Mere Christianity*, pp 130-131.

b. Headship does *not* mean set roles or jobs in the house

The headship-and-submission idea doesn't lock in any particular roles for husband and wife. It's not as if he has to look after the money and she has to do all the cooking. In my marriage, Kathy is brilliant with money and I'm hopeless (although she's a great cook, too). Unfortunately, when we moved into our current house we inherited a swimming pool (which means 52 weeks of maintenance for 52 minutes of swimming). Kathy is the chemist and brains of the filter and water quality, while I'm the pool boy and labourer. I mainly look after our social diary, but she's got the bank balance covered. It all comes down to who's gifted at what.

What about the house-husband thing—you staying at home to look after the kids while your wife works full-time as the main 'breadwinner'? I'll come back to that in the next section on love and respect. In the meantime, I'll put a few more cats into the bag to stick my head in.

c. Headship *does* mean love and respect

Notice that the apostle Paul shows the husband and wife needing different things from each other. The roles and the partners in marriage are equal, but they are not interchangeable.

In his excellent book *Love and Respect*, Emerson Eggerichs explains these differences, which the apostle Paul spells out so clearly.[13] As verse 33 in the Ephesians passage above shows, she needs to know she is loved and secure; he wants respect more than anything, especially from his wife (as well as other people). Incidentally, the word for respect in verse 33, *phobos*, can be translated as 'respect', 'reverence' or even 'awe'—so it could possibly be translated to say that wives should consider their husbands as 'awesome'. But maybe we shouldn't push it with our

---

13 E Eggerichs, *Love and Respect: The love she most desires; the respect he desperately needs*, Thomas Nelson, 2004.

wives—they know us too well.

In the first half of *Love and Respect*, Dr Eggerichs speaks about "the crazy cycle". That is, when a wife is feeling unloved, she is likely to react by not showing her husband respect, which means he may react by withdrawing and not showing her love, which reinforces the downward cycle. The second half of the book shows the opposite, positive upward spiral: "the energizing cycle". When he loves her and she feels loved, she is more likely to give him the respect he needs, and so he's more likely to love her.

I like this book because you don't have to read between the lines; Eggerichs helps us blokes by giving simple, clear ideas about how to love your wife. He does it under the acronym COUPLE:

- Closeness: she wants you to be close
- Openness: she wants you to open up to her
- Understanding: don't try to fix her; just listen
- Peacemaking: she wants you to say "I'm sorry"
- Loyalty: she needs to know you're committed
- Esteem: she wants you to honour and cherish her

Now, to return to the house-husband issue. I don't think the Bible gives a direct command on this issue, but there are patterns of marriage and family life. I say this mostly at the level of 'this is my opinion' based on many years of observation. No doubt people will disagree, which is their right, of course. You will have to make up your own mind. With that said, here's my view: it's possible to arrange a marriage so that the husband stays home as primary carer and the wife is the breadwinner working outside the home; but, given the way men and women are wired, it's not easy to make this work long-term. Women are more naturally wired up to be nurturing of little kids. I submit the ability to breastfeed as one clear piece of evidence. Breastfeeding and the production of oxytocin (the 'cuddle hormone') are linked.[14] There are also the more feminine characteristics identified in Alan Medinger's book (mentioned in chapter 2), which tend to predominate in women and which gravitate towards the role of primary caregiving.

At the same time, becoming a new dad actually changes a man's brain, helping him bond with his baby.[15] But the issue is not the dad's ability or desire to bond with his children; it's the question of respect from his wife. Can a wife continue to respect her husband as head of the house when she goes to work each day and is the main income earner? I've seen this done by a couple who are friends of mine, and it worked because of the particular gift mix of the couple and the jobs they both did. They managed it for several years, and the marriage worked just fine. But I've also seen the reverse: the house-husband arrangement undermined the dynamics of the marriage and the respect for the husband declined. Leonard Sax, an American doctor and author, is in favour of the move to house husbands, but explains that the lived experience of many couples makes him sceptical, or at least cautious, about recommending the arrangement.[16]

I've watched this issue play out for a long time, and I'd say it is possible to make the house-husband thing work. But it's most certainly swimming against the natural (i.e. God-created) current in male/female relationships, particularly considering headship and submission as defined above, and it will require hard work. In fact, the longer it continues, the more work will be required to

---

14 "Oxytocin also has important psychological effects, and is known to affect mothering behaviour in animals. In humans, oxytocin induces a state of calm, and reduces stress. It may enhance feelings of affection between mother and child, and promote bonding" (World Health Organization, *Infant and Young Child Feeding: Model chapter for textbooks for medical students and allied health professionals*, WHO, 2009, p 12, accessed 7 January 2022 [who.int/publications/i/item/9789241597494]).

15 Farrell and Gray, *The Boy Crisis*, pp 110-111.

16 Sax, *Boys Adrift*, p 165.

keep the respect and love happening. It's a tough road to sign up for long-term.

Some simple, practical advice from 40 years of working at it

As I said, this short chapter isn't in any way comprehensive. If you want to go deeper, there are lots of good books around on marriage. I've read a few, and I've had several read to me in bed. There are also many good courses to strengthen marriages (see my recommendations at the end of the chapter).

I want to share with you some pieces of marriage gold that I've learned over my 40 years on the job. Of course, I'm still trying to become a better husband.

a. Love her as *she* wants to be loved

In his book *The 5 Love Languages*, Gary Chapman stresses the importance of actually showing your spouse love in the way they will receive it. Chapman says people receive or perceive love in different ways.[17] It's possible to be trying to show someone love, but to do so in such a way that they won't see it or receive it because what you're doing doesn't register with them. The concrete examples are quite clear. He lists five different ways in which marriage partners receive or perceive love. These are: words of affirmation; quality time; receiving gifts; acts of service; and physical touch.

Let's expand on these a little further:

- Words of affirmation: these are simple statements like words of encouragement, appreciation and approval.
- Quality time: this involves giving your full, undivided atten-

17 G Chapman, *The 5 Love Languages: The secret to love that lasts,* Moody Press, 2016.

tion to the other person and actually listening and talking with them. It doesn't fill someone's love tank if you're multitasking on your phone or watching TV.

- Receiving gifts: some people are naturally tuned to appreciate symbols of love more than anything else. They don't have to be expensive, just thoughtful.
- Acts of service: this comes down to actually serving your spouse by doing things like housework. By serving them in whatever capacity, they will feel deeply loved.
- Physical touch: for some people, touching will provide a greater feeling of security and love within the relationship than anything else you can do for them. This isn't the same thing as sex; it's a physical touch of affection, like holding hands or giving a big hug, or an arm around the shoulder.

Discovering your wife's love language (or languages) is a key part of a successful marriage—and you need to help her know your own love language(s), too. Love is a daily choice, not always a feeling. Loving feelings sometimes aren't there, but you can still decide to be loving. Keep practising it, even when it's uncomfortable or doesn't feel natural.

b. It's your job to take the spiritual initiative in your home

Get into the right routines with your wife—pray and read the Bible. For the man who follows Jesus, there's no greater priority than reading the Bible and praying with your wife, and yet so many blokes I've spoken to don't do that. It's not hard; you pick a book of the Bible, you sit down together, and you read a part of it with her. It can be a few verses, or half a chapter, or more if you want. Then share your thoughts on that part of the Bible. They don't have to be the musings of Billy Graham or Charles Spurgeon; just talk with her about what you think this part of the Bible is saying to you both. If you're not sure, then that's something to think about for the rest of the day. And then pray with her. Here's how it goes at our place:

Me: Anything we should pray about?

Kathy: Yep. [insert 2 or 3 wise things to pray about]

Me: Would you like to pray?

Kathy: No, you should lead, you're the dad. [This totally depends on what makes your wife comfortable; I'm just telling you what Kathy says.]

Me: You sure?

Kathy: Yep.

I'll then pray about the things we mentioned, and Kathy usually prays at the end about something I missed or didn't fully cover.

There are so many good reasons to do this. Primarily, we need to hear from God together, and God answers prayers. That's obviously enough reason right there. But as well as that, this little event each day will keep you close to each other. Prayer is intimate and personal, an essential activity to do with your wife.

By the way, that's why you shouldn't pray one-to-one in private with another woman. I know I sound weird, but prayer *is* intimate, and it's unwise to be emotionally or personally intimate with a woman who is not your wife. I know there'll be exceptions—for example, what if she's old enough to be your mum? But you know the heart of what I'm saying here. Be wise.

When do you read the Bible with your wife and pray together? Whenever it works. Build it into the routine of your life. We have a Bible beside the dinner table. After dinner each night, I open the Bible to read a small part, and then we pray. We've done this for 37 years, since our eldest daughter was born. Maybe for you it could be after breakfast, or before bed, or whenever works in your routine. If you don't have kids (yet), it's a good idea to get into that routine before kids arrive. After kids arrive, you need to read with the whole family—all the kids! (It gets hard, but it can be done.) But you still should be reading and praying with your wife alone.

One other thing: when you take the lead on this, if your wife is a follower of Jesus, she will *love* it. She will love that you care for her and that you are taking the spiritual lead in the marriage. So many Christian women long for their husbands to take the lead with Bible reading and prayer. Don't worry if you've been married for years and haven't been doing this; make the decision to start fresh. Talk to your wife and work out a regular time in your routine together. You can begin with just a few minutes. Read any part of the Bible and pray with her. It will be good for both of you spiritually, and your wife will love that you're taking the initiative.

If you are a follower of Jesus and your wife isn't yet, I know that's tough. Your mission is to love her just the same, and you should stay with her (as we saw in the previous chapter; see 1 Corinthians 7:12-13). To love her and model Jesus' love to her is the most powerful thing you can do to open her ears to hear the message of Jesus. (The apostle Peter outlines a similar idea for wives who are married to husbands who aren't yet followers of Jesus; see 1 Peter 3:1-2.)

It's tough being married to someone who doesn't share your deepest commitment. I don't say that as a cliché; I grew up in a home where one parent was a committed follower of Jesus and the other was not. I saw firsthand that this wasn't easy for either of them. But be assured that your wife is watching you, and living a life of integrity as you follow Jesus will give great credibility to your words about him.

c. Creating the intimacy where a marriage thrives

Sex within a marriage is about bonding and intimacy. This is a relationship that husband and wife can and should share with no-one else; it is a special intimacy. That is why pornography is poison (actually, this is just one of the many reasons it's poison): it separates the sex act from relational intimacy. In pornography, sex becomes something you do to someone, rather than a profound form of intimacy that you share in the safe context of a lifetime commitment.

So the question really is: how do you build that intimacy in a marriage? How do you get emotionally close to her so that the two of you can enjoy that physical intimacy? Sex is obviously good fun, and it's also good for your relationship. It's the glue that will hold you together. That's why the apostle Paul actually commands married couples to meet each other's physical needs for sexual intimacy:

> The husband should fulfil his marital duty to his wife, and likewise the wife to her husband. The wife does not have authority over her own body but yields it to her husband. In the same way, the husband does not have authority over his own body but yields it to his wife. Do not deprive each other except perhaps by mutual consent and for a time, so that you may devote yourselves to prayer. Then come together again so that Satan will not tempt you because of your lack of self-control. (1 Cor 7:3-5)

Here are three key ideas to help create and keep sexual intimacy within your marriage: be nice to your wife; smell good for your wife; and plan ahead for your wife.

i. Be nice to your wife

In his popular *Laugh Your Way to a Better Marriage* seminar, Mark Gungor talks about the importance of simple acts of kindness.[18] There are simple things a husband can do that tell his wife he loves her. Some of them may not even take a lot of effort. For example, you get out of bed, then you make the bed. It takes two or three minutes, but it tells her that you care. Clean up your clothes off the floor, or empty the dishwasher. There are lots of little jobs, but they add up. As you pull your weight with housework, it lifts weight off her.

On this, I actually agree with Clementine Ford. You're not 'helping out'; you're doing what you should and pulling your weight around the house:

> It isn't 'helping' to do a handful of chores in a house *you live in*. 'Helping' is when you go around to your mate's place for a working bee or provide the answer to a hard crossword clue. It isn't 'doing less than your equal share and patting yourself on the back for being such a Good Guy'. Everyone, no matter what their gender, needs to stop framing men's contributions to the domestic workload as 'helping'. All this does is position that workload as belonging to women, with anything done by men an unexpected act of generosity that deserves acknowledgement and praise.[19]

In many 21st-century households, the wife is not just working full-time but running the house pretty much on her own. Being useless around the house breeds resentment with your lady, and there's nothing more likely to kill the passion in your marriage. Bettina Arndt knows, and she's one of the few female commentators in the man's corner when it comes to this issue:

> That's the crux of the sex–housework issue. Yes, women are understandably resentful when they feel their partners

18 See laughyourway.com.
19 Ford, *Boys Will Be Boys,* p 58 (emphasis original).

aren't sharing their second shift. Why should they put out and 'just do it', if their partners aren't prepared to consider their needs and pull their own weight when it comes to the relentless burden of housework and childcare? The resentment these women feel is often a sure-fire passion killer.[20]

I have improved over the years, but I still have a way to go. So do your share of the washing, tidying, dishwasher stacking and unpacking. By the way, I'm not beating up on blokes. Bettina Arndt has some interesting stats that show men work longer hours in paid work, and if you combine paid work and housework, men and women do about the same.[21]

I know you'll have heard this before; other people have told you to help with the housework. But this next part is gold—something that will make you a Jedi master as a husband. This is vital! Ready? When you do housework, *do not draw her attention to it*. Just do it, and don't mention what you've done. Got it? This is important. If you draw attention to what you have done, the jobs will have no value. In fact, it may even be negative. Why? Because she wants you to be an adult member of the team. Doing housework is not scoring points with her; it's actually just pulling your weight around the house as a fellow adult. Teenagers need to be nagged and reminded and praised; adults pull their weight and don't need to draw attention to their contributions.

---

20 Arndt, *#MenToo*, p 184.

21 "It's fascinating that the household issue so often gets a run whenever there is any criticism of women's behaviour. And even here the 'truth' regarding men's participation in household work rarely gets a hearing. Just after I published *The Sex Diaries*, it was widely reported that the latest social trends survey found that women do almost twice as much housework as men—33 hours and 45 minutes a week. What the media failed to mention was men spend a lot more time in paid jobs—an average of 31 hours and 15 minutes a week, compared with women's 16 hours and 25 minutes. In other words, men and women do about the same amount of work in total—about 50 hours a week each. How is it that we never hear this side of the story?" (Arndt, *#MenToo*, pp 184-185).

Now, you may be thinking: "But what if she doesn't notice?" Relax; she will notice. From what I've heard and observed, most women could be members of the CSI team: they're far more observant than the average male. It's when you do housework without drawing attention to it—when you get on and do what you should be doing anyway without requesting or expecting any credit for it—that she will truly appreciate it. Trust me.

In fact, if you're worrying about whether she'll notice, maybe the penny still hasn't dropped: don't do these things to get noticed; do them because it's the right thing to do.

ii. Smell good for your wife

You may not realize it, but your wife, as a woman, has a much better sense of smell than you have as a man. In fact, she has almost double the neurons dedicated to being able to smell in the olfactory bulb in her brain. Women average 6.9 million neurons compared to the average man with 3.5 million.[22] So when she says you smell bad, she's right in two ways: (1) your nose is not as effective at identifying unpleasant smells, and (2) you need a shower. Compared with you, your wife has the sense of smell of a bloodhound. If you want the idea of sex to be appealing for her, you need to smell good. That means you should have a shower even when you think you don't need it. Brush your teeth, even if you don't think you need to. Mouthwash? Yes. Even brush your

---

22 Time for a quick anatomy lesson. Smell receptors in the nose send their signals via the olfactory nerve to the olfactory bulb. The olfactory bulb is located on the bottom side of the brain. The olfactory bulb is the first stop for information about smell. There are two kinds of cells in the brain: neurons and glial cells. Neurons are considered the most important, because they seem to play the most important role in sending information via electrical signals. But glial cells are essential too, because they provide structure and may also modulate information processing in the brain. On all counts, women beat men: cells in the olfactory bulb (16.2 million for the average woman, compared with 9.2 million for the average man); neurons in the olfactory bulb (6.9 million to 3.5 million); and glial cells (9.3 million to 5.7 million). All of these differences are highly statistically significant. See Sax, *Why Gender Matters*, p 16.

tongue with toothpaste and toothbrush. If you doubt me, just try it and see how much it helps.

I know that seems like very specific advice, but the little things matter. Over the course of decades of your married life together, they all add up. Show your wife that you love and care for her by the way you approach the little things—including how you look after yourself and how you look after the house.

iii. Plan for your wife

In the busyness of life, couples easily get tired and overrun, and sex can get squeezed out of an overly busy schedule. For your wife, it's likely that things need to be calm and in place, because women tend to think globally about everything that is going on, whereas we men tend to focus only on what is in front of us. We can have tunnel vision. The average woman may be less inclined towards sex if the house feels chaotic because there's a whole lot of housework not done; the average man can feel like sex in the middle of a tornado.

This means it's important that we think ahead. Be prepared to take the initiative. And I don't mean saying "You awake, love?" in the middle of the night. When I say you should take the initiative, I mean you should work hard to create the space and time so she can feel connected to you and feel emotionally intimate with you, first and foremost.

I must confess to often being lazy with this myself. But occasionally I've got it right. When our children were little and life was frantic, I would plan a night or even a couple of days away with Kathy two or three times a year. It was a great opportunity to leave the kids with someone we trusted and have some quality time together, including the kind of marital intimacy that so easily gets squeezed out in the midst of nappies, vomit and busyness. Planning three months ahead is great, where possible; but making the effort in the midst of a busy week to plan some quiet time for her to gather her thoughts (you might call it 'me time' for her) can be a big help.

How would you arrange for her to feel like she's in love with you? Think about some simple acts of kindness, as well as opportunities to go out to places she likes. Or look after the kids so she can go out somewhere with friends (or on her own). I don't mean you should do this just to have sex, but that intimacy will often follow when you care for her in this way (because you do actually care for her!). How would you think that through for today, or for this week?

One other thing that's important: don't take the whole sex thing too seriously. That is, if it doesn't work out on a particular occasion, don't get huffy and overly precious about it. This just gives you the opportunity to re-plan, to take the initiative to care for her, and to make room for intimacy with her for next time.

In many marriages, the wife is not the one to initiate sex as she may not have a particularly high level of desire. It's easy to understand why, especially if she has young children and she's working part-time or full-time. It's your job as a husband to initiate intimacy, to lovingly pursue her, and to create the circumstances in which she will feel like being intimate. Whatever happens, don't get discouraged. Don't confuse a lack of desire to initiate with a lack of passion once things get started. Don't give up; it may take some patience, especially if you have small children.

In summary, many men have the energy for the physical act of sex, but they're lazy when it comes to creating the opportunities, the environment and the mood in which she will feel like sex. The challenge is to man up and take the initiative to create the circumstances in which your wife will feel like being especially intimate with you. It takes work, but the rewards (for both of you) are more than worth it.

Of course, sex is one important sign of an intimate, healthy marriage. But to focus only on sex is to miss the main issue:

talking with her, listening to her, spending time with her, making the effort to understand her, and loving her in practical, insightful ways. These are the things that will bring real intimacy to your marriage. These are also the things that take emotional effort. Sex is good, but it flows out of other kinds of real intimacy you can share with your wife. It's an intimacy that, God willing, you'll have a lifetime to develop.

Eight recommended books on marriage

- *Married for God: Making your marriage the best it can be* by Christopher Ash
- *The 5 Love Languages: The secret to love that lasts* by Gary Chapman
- *When Sinners Say "I Do": Discovering the power of the gospel for marriage* by Dave Harvey
- *Friends and Lovers: Cultivating companionship and intimacy in marriage* by Joel R Beeke
- *Love and Respect: The love she most desires; the respect he desperately needs* by Emerson Eggerichs
- *The Seven Principles for Making Marriage Work: A practical guide from the country's foremost relationship expert* by John Gottman
- *Bringing Out the Best in Your Wife: Encourage your spouse and experience the relationship you've always wanted* by H Norman Wright
- *The Meaning of Marriage: Facing the complexities of commitment with the wisdom of God* by Timothy and Kathy Keller (for something more theologically in-depth)

Three recommended marriage courses

- *Building a Safe and Strong Marriage* by Keith and Sarah Condie: buildingmarriage.com.au
- *Laugh Your Way to a Better Marriage* by Mark Gungor: markgungor.com/products/laugh-your-way-to-a-better-marriage-1
- *The Marriage Course* by Nicky and Sila Lee: themarriagecourse.org

12. MAN UP AS A FATHER

"Parenthood remains the single greatest preserve
of the amateur."
—Alvin Toffler

THERE WAS A TIME when I could carry all four of my children at once: one piggyback, one on my chest, and one in each arm. Now my son could carry me around no problem, and eventually I suppose together they will choose my nursing home.

Being a dad is a great thing. For most men, their kids generate a whole range of emotions they never expected they could feel so strongly. My strongest emotions, both positive and negative, have come through my children. In fact, there are actual changes that take place in the brain of a new dad. He will begin producing more oxytocin—a hormone that stimulates nurturing, trust and affection—to encourage bonding with his new offspring.[1]

As those of you with adult kids will have experienced, "At some stage your children begin to outpace you, become smarter, quicker, stronger, sometimes wiser. ... Fatherhood can easily be the best thing you do in your life."[2] For many men, there's great joy in seeing kids grow up, in being with them as they turn into young adults. But for other men, there's the heartache of not being able to have kids or, perhaps even worse, not being able to

1   Farrell and Gray, *The Boy Crisis,* pp 110-111.
2   Biddulph, *The New Manhood,* p 145.

have access to your own kids because of family breakdown. I don't have any easy answers for this. I've talked to a lot of men about this stuff, and I know it's really tough not to have all the access to your kids that you'd want.

With four children (three daughters and a son, all now adults), I have some experience being a dad. (I also have three grandchildren, which is great fun—in fact, it's all fun and very little responsibility. Hang in there for eventually being a grandad. It's worth it!) But while I've had some experience, I certainly don't consider myself an expert. I expect most parents would quietly confess that often they are scratching their heads and making it up as they go. As author James Dobson quips, "I used to have four theories on child-rearing and no kids. I now have four kids and no theories."[3]

Why is this? One reason is that every child is different. Some kids arrive in the world and ask for the rulebook so they can work out how to be compliant in every way. Others climb from the womb and ask for the rulebook so they can set fire to it (or smoke the pages). Every kid is different, and so treating them fairly can mean treating kids differently. For example, you may need to discipline two kids in different ways for the discipline to be effective. Kids mature at different stages, and so what they are able or allowed to do at different ages may not be the same. Having said all that, don't show favouritism in the family. The quickest way to put bitterness into a kid's heart is to play favourites.

So, there you go; simple, really—you probably need to treat them differently in order to be fair, but don't show favouritism whatever you do.

Confused? Welcome to being a dad.

Anyway, let me give you a few thoughts on fatherhood. I know there have been volumes written on the subject. But for what it's

3   Quoted in C Ash, *Job: The Wisdom of the Cross*, Crossway, 2014, p 94.

worth, here's a summary of 37 years of my thinking, my mistakes, and the occasional win, as well as a gold nugget from the Bible.

Charting the long course

I'm not a good swimmer. I probably should have known better than to enter an ocean-swimming race at Bondi Beach. It was a biathlon, with a swim of about one kilometre then a run of about 5 km. By the time we were 'out the back' behind the waves, I had dropped off the pack and was falling further and further behind. But I was going okay—head down, stroke, stroke, stroke. Next thing I knew, two lifesavers roared up beside me in a rubber ducky.[4] One of them leaned over and shouted at me, "Hey mate, you better straighten up. Have a look: you're headed for New Zealand!" (Given that New Zealand is a bit over 2,000 km away, it was good advice. Don't keep swimming east from Bondi.) I was busy swimming, but I hadn't been getting my head up and looking for the marker buoys showing the course.

Being a dad can be a bit like that. Day by day, with busyness, and tiredness, and getting food in their mouths and clothes on their backs, stroke, stroke, stroke, we just keep going. But we need to get our heads up and see the marker buoys. What's the long-term course we're charting for our kids? Are we going in the right direction, or have we drifted off course?

Here's where I think you'll see the most important marker buoys: your aim should be to move your children from having no responsibility, no decisions and no consequences when they're babies, to being young adults with the wisdom to make decisions that have adult consequences. As toddlers, they know nothing and decide nothing; they have some mobility, but no brains and no consequences. As young adults, your kids are likely to get

4   A small, inflatable boat with an outboard motor, used for surf rescue.

behind the wheel of a tonne of steel that's potentially lethal, and they will be able to drink, or smoke, or ingest whatever they choose. They will choose who they spend time with, where (or whether) they work or study, where they live, and plenty of other major and minor decisions. They'll live with the consequences of their choices. You have maybe 18 years to prepare them for all that. No pressure! You need to keep your eyes on the big picture.

The difference a dad makes

There's lots of advice around for dads—some good, some not so good. Here's a brilliant instruction from the New Testament, coming in at just 18 words: "Fathers, do not exasperate your children; instead, bring them up in the training and instruction of the Lord" (Eph 6:4).[5] Three really important things jump out from this verse.

First, did you notice that *Paul writes directly to the fathers*? Although it's not politically correct, God expects fathers to lead and be the head of their families. This is not the authority of some tin-pot dictator, but an authority that comes with the responsibility of sacrificially loving, leading and looking after your family. If you have kids, you cannot just hand over the raising of your children to your wife. It's a partnership—something you have to do together. In fact, God expects you to take the lead in caring for your family. And that means you've got to be around. You have to *be present in your children's lives*. You know your own dad's example in this was important for good or ill. Present or absent, dads have a huge effect on kids.

In *The New Manhood*, Steve Biddulph says: "A good dad makes

---

5   The Bible obviously talks about the role of mothers in raising, teaching and disciplining children (e.g. Prov 1:8: "Listen, my son, to your father's instruction and do not forsake your mother's teaching"). Yet it is instructive that Paul singles out fathers; we have this responsibility, and often we need reminding.

the family feel safe in the world. A bad one makes the family feel afraid, mostly of him."[6] Dads are not simply an optional extra in raising kids. You have a massive influence on your child. The experts and lived experience all confirm this. As a psychologist, Biddulph gives a summary of his findings on the effect of having dad present in a child's life:

> Not all dads are a positive influence in their children's lives, but on average given a half-decent male trying to do his best, the benefits might really shock you. The research picture is stunningly clear. If there is a father in the home, then statistically:

- both boys and girls have higher self-esteem
- they both do better in school, and stay on in school longer
- they become better qualified and more likely to be employed
- they are less likely to have trouble with the law
- they are less likely to be victims of assault, rape, sexual abuse
- girls are less likely to experience early sexual intercourse or teen pregnancy
- boys are less likely to be violent or belong to a gang, and
- boys and girls are less likely to have problems with drugs or alcohol.[7]

If you want to drill down further on the importance of having a dad around, Warren Farrell and John Gray devote 60 pages of their book *The Boy Crisis* to discussing why a dad being present is so important in the lives of their sons. They list 15 positive ways that a dad can influence his boy's life. These include physical and mental wellbeing, eventual employment, and even the

---

6   Biddulph, *The New Manhood*, p 152.
7   Biddulph, *The New Manhood*, p 147.

likelihood of going to prison.[8]

Dads need to be around. There has been a huge increase in single-parent families in Western nations over the last couple of generations, and the vast majority of these are single women working to raise kids. In Australia, the Australian Council of Social Service (ACOSS) has said that these single-mum families are three times more likely than other families to live below the poverty line.[9]

Recognizing the cost of children growing up without a father in the house is still being resisted in Australia. But in the USA, after decades of denial, the cost of fatherlessness is finally being acknowledged. Former President Barack Obama, himself the product of a single-mother family, was particularly vocal about the problem in "the African-American community", where more than 70 percent of children are born to unmarried mothers:[10]

8   Farrell and Gray's 15 benefits for children who have active and involved dads are: (1) better academic achievement; (2) increased verbal and mathematical abilities; (3) lower likelihood of dropping out of school; (4) higher likelihood of employment as a young adult; (5) greatly reduced risk of childhood or teenage suicide; (6) significantly lower risk of drug addiction or other drug problems; (7) much lower likelihood of homelessness (90 percent of runaways or homeless youth are from fatherless homes); (8) significantly lower rates of being bullied or being a bully; (9) much less likelihood of experiencing child abuse, violence, sexual assault and domestic violence; (10) reduction in violent crime; (11) far lower likelihood of committing sexual assault (80 percent of rapists come from fatherless homes); (12) reduced levels of poverty; (13) reduced hypertension; (14) greater ability to form open, receptive and trusting relationships with new people in their lives; (15) greater ability to empathize with other people in adulthood; see Farrell and Gray, *The Boy Crisis*, pp 118-119 and 402-407. This is mostly based on research in America, but the point applies much more widely; for example, Steve Biddulph stresses the same kinds of ideas in his book about raising girls (*Raising Girls in the Twenty-First Century: From babyhood to womanhood—helping your daughter to grow up wise, strong and free*, Simon & Schuster, 2019).

9   L Henriques-Gomes, "'It's soul destroying": The stress and stigma of being a single parent on welfare', *The Guardian*, 19 April 2019, accessed 7 January 2022 (theguardian.com/australia-news/2019/apr/19/its-soul-destroying-the-stress-and-stigma-of-being-a-single-parent-on-welfare).

10   J Chamie, 'Out-of-wedlock births rise worldwide', *YaleGlobal Online*, 16 March 2017, accessed 7 January 2022 (archive-yaleglobal.yale.edu/content/out-wedlock-births-rise-worldwide).

We know the statistics—that children who grow up without a father are five times more likely to live in poverty and commit crime, nine times more likely to drop out of schools and 20 times more likely to end up in prison. They are more likely to have behavioral problems or run away from home or become teenage parents themselves. And the foundations of our community are weaker because of it.[11]

It's not just that the father of a child needs to be around; research says that the stability of 'married parents' makes a significant difference, compared to the instability of de facto relationships. This is not to say that all de facto relationships are unstable compared to all marriages. But in the wider analysis, marriage relationships are much more likely to last.[12]

With this in mind, here's one thing that's worth remembering but which can feel counterintuitive: don't make your kids the centre or total focus of family life. The best thing you can do for your kids is to keep your marriage strong and healthy. (There's a very thoughtful extended testimony from a divorced dad at the end of this chapter; I can only imagine how tough this can be.) Kids really want to know if life is secure, if the home base is safe. If mum and dad are strong and together and their relationship comes first within family life, it provides the safe home base that kids long for. Importantly, this continues even after kids have become adults and left home.

Dads are needed early in life, not just when the little ones start walking and talking. In fact, they're needed even earlier. I know you were present at the conception.[13] But a dad's presence is vital especially in the early development of a child. Farrell and Gray have a long list of the stages where a dad is vital, from even

11   Quoted in Arndt, *#MenToo*, p 247.
12   Arndt, *#MenToo*, p 247.
13   Of course, this is not always true—for example, in the case of adoptive fathers.

before conception through to preschool. They suggest: "Ironically, of all the years that children need their dads, perhaps the tender years [i.e. preschool] are most important".[14] It's also a sad fact that children, particularly girls, are safer with their biological father in the house. Arndt notes:

> Turn on the ABC News and every few days there's another report on institutional child sexual abuse. Yet the chances of being felt up by a horny priest or YMCA childcare worker are mighty slim compared to the numbers of children at risk from mum's boyfriend. A report by Jeremy Sammut from the Centre for Independent Studies reviewed more than seventy research studies to provide overwhelming evidence that girls are sexually abused by 'stepfathers'—partners of their single, remarried or re-partnered mothers—at up to 20 times the rate of abuse by biological fathers.[15]

If I can push a little further, dads need to be not just sleeping at home and putting in a cameo appearance now and then; they have to actually be present and involved in the lives of their kids. I know it's tough to work, to earn enough money to feed and clothe and house your family, and there's pressure at work, and often your employer wants more and more hours. But if I had my time over again, I would spend more time with my kids when they were little. I urge you to not let your work crowd out your time with them. They are only little for a short time. Steve Biddulph has some wise words that may be hard to hear:

> Your work can be a danger to your family. What children get from a career father is not his happiness, nor his teaching, nor his substance, but only the leftover scraps of his life and, mostly, his mood. And at 7 o'clock at night, that mood

14 Farrell and Gray, *The Boy Crisis*, pp 126-127.
15 Arndt, *#MenToo*, p 254.

is often irritation and fatigue. Work, parenthood, couple time and self-time are four legs of your life, and it takes real grace and a conscious choice to keep them all strong. Both boys and girls need fathers who are around, but for boys it can be critical. It's likely that boys are programmed to need several hours of male contact every day. This can come from school teachers, scout leaders and sports coaches but for the most part, most days, this means you.[16]

Someone will fill those little heads with values, with a way of seeing the world, with right and wrong. Don't you want to be the one programming the software?

I reckon every young dad should be made to listen to Harry Chapin's song 'Cat's in the Cradle' once a week.[17] Okay, maybe once a month. Very briefly, it's the story of a dad who is always too busy to spend time with his son. Yet the young son still idolizes his dad and longs to grow up just like him. But the second half of the song describes the grown-up son who is, of course, too busy to spend time with his aging father. He's grown up just like his dad. It's a real tearjerker that puts the cold hand of guilt onto the heart of all dads. Every time I've listened to it, I've felt that guilt—except for once, when it came on the radio as I was driving home from an overnight canoeing trip with my son. I thought, "Yes! Just once I have beaten you, Harry!" The song might be a cruel and unusual torture, but it calls on us loud and clear to make time for our kids. Chances are they will grow up to be just like us.

16 Biddulph, *The New Manhood*, p 154.
17 You can find the lyrics online at *The Harry Chapin Archive* (harrychapin.com/music/cats.shtml).

Train and instruct, don't exasperate

In a father–child relationship, power moves from one side of the relationship to the other. When children are toddlers, parents basically have all the power. You decide when they will see you, where they go, what they wear, and what they eat. True, you can't decide what mood they're in as they do it, or how much food actually gets in their mouths at any one time. But with a bit of persistence (and appropriate use of seatbelts) you have pretty good control over them.

But by the time your offspring are young adults, the power balance has moved dramatically. It is now shared. They make most of their own decisions. If they're young males and still at home, on weekends they'll have one meal per day: it starts about 8 am and concludes about 9 pm. If they've moved out of home, they choose where they go and what they eat. You negotiate together when you'll see each other, make suggestions about what they wear, and offer to provide food as an incentive to get together. But remember that just a few decades down the track, the power will be almost all theirs. They'll be choosing your nursing home and your walking frame.

So here is the *second* key truth from Ephesians 6: dads, *be aware of the power you have, especially when children are young.* Be careful not to misuse it: "Fathers, *do not exasperate your children ...*"

I said earlier on that as you train and instruct over many years, you move your children from having no responsibility, no decisions and no consequences to being young adults with responsibility for making their own decisions, and to being people who are aware of the consequences of these decisions. Obviously love, affection, affirmation and encouragement are vitally important in that process. But so is discipline, and that needs to start early. Little kids are basically savages (cute, but still savages) who need to be socialized. The earlier you start, the better. It's too late when they're bigger than you. Actually, it's too late long before that.

a. Start early, while you can ...

Here's Jordan Peterson's list of things a child needs to learn early so they can socialize with other people:

> Do not bite, kick or hit, except in self-defence. Do not torture and bully other children, so you don't end up in jail. Eat in a civilized and thankful manner, so that people are happy to have you at their house, and pleased to feed you. Learn to share, so other kids will play with you. Pay attention when spoken to by adults, so they don't hate you and might therefore deign to teach you something. Go to sleep properly, and peaceably, so that your parents can have a private life and not resent your existence. Take care of your belongings, because you need to learn how and because you're lucky to have them. Be good company when something fun is happening, so that you're invited for the fun. Act so that other people are happy you're around, so that people will want you around. A child who knows these rules will be welcome everywhere.[18]

"Training and instruction" isn't about punishing a child, but preparing a child to deal with reality and relationships—or, if you prefer, preparing them to deal with the consequences of their decisions for other people.

b. Tying actions to consequences

Part of disciplining our kids includes helping them to see the connection between their actions and the consequences of those actions—and letting them experience those consequences. If you

18 Peterson, *12 Rules for Life*, p 137.

don't discipline your children in this way (in a way that is age-appropriate and carefully managed by you, of course), it will inevitably end in disaster. In the Old Testament, Eli the Priest and King David were both hopeless as dads—they didn't discipline their sons (see 1 Sam 2-4; 2 Sam 13-14; 1 Kgs 1:6). This resulted in tragedy for their sons and their families, and indeed for all of Israel.

If children grow up and have not felt consequences, they can be immature as adults—even dangerous to themselves and others.[19] Biddulph has further good advice in this regard:

> Discipline works by cooperation. Natural consequences and a sense of fairness are your tools. Negotiate with him. So as a toddler, not too many consequences because they're just babies. But as they grow up you slowly introduce age-appropriate consequences for actions. You can't make a teenager do things by force—but you provide so many services that your bargaining power is huge.[20]

Let me give you an example: the teenage boy plays football on the weekend, and his mother agrees that she will wash all his football gear—jersey, shorts and socks. Boy is instructed to unroll dirty socks, stretch them out, and put them near the washing machine. Boy does not unroll socks, but leaves them rolled up like sweaty, muddy donuts, where he has just rolled them off his shins, and leaves them thrown on the floor in the laundry. Mum finds them week after week, complains to you (dad), and also complains to said boy, and then she washes the socks. Boy wears the clean socks the following week. Mum wonders why boy's behaviour will not change despite being reminded. Dad gets grief

19 See M Balson, *Becoming Better Parents,* The Australian Council for Educational Research, 1981.
20 S Biddulph, *Raising Boys in the Twenty-First Century: How to help our boys become open-hearted, kind and strong men,* rev edn, HarperCollins, 2018, p 109.

about this on an ongoing basis.

Then wise dad reads *The Manual* and says to boy (after prior discussion with mum), "Son, from now on if you do not put your socks in the correct place and in the right condition, the socks will not be washed". Boy ignores the decree, and the following Saturday morning he finds not a beautifully washed pair of socks, but two sweaty, muddy donuts still sitting on the laundry floor. Boy then unrolls and wears sweaty, muddy donuts. Come the end of the football game, boy either does the right thing with the socks and they are washed, or another round of the donut game ensues. Either way, dad has taken the initiative and cared for his wife as he should. Boy has a decision to make: muddy donuts or clean socks.

In one sense this is a trivial example, but the consequences are built into the action. You can nag him all you want, but while mum is washing his socks regardless, he's not listening to her. This can apply to all kinds of things: packing to go somewhere, doing homework, study and exam preparation, saving money for a holiday, or even something as simple as coming to the dinner table when called.

Now, I'm not saying this will work perfectly, but the more closely we can tie the activity (or wrongdoing or right-doing) to the flow-on consequences of the action, the quicker the child will learn how they should act; reality is the teacher. As I said, it must be age-appropriate. So the 3-year-old who forgets to take his or her lunch to preschool should probably get a special delivery that day, but the 15-year-old who forgets lunch probably only needs to go hungry once or twice to jog his or her memory.

I'll say once again and for the last time, this isn't easy. It will take a lot of wisdom, and it doesn't always work across every different issue. But it's the right marker buoy to have in mind in the great ocean-swim of child-raising.

One of the reasons dads make such a difference in family life is that they are more likely to enforce boundaries. As Farrell and Gray say, "Teaching a child to treat boundaries seriously teaches him or her to respect the needs of others".[21]

c. Anger doesn't motivate

One more thing about disciplining—and this is brilliant. I learned it from James Dobson of Focus on the Family:[22] "Anger doesn't motivate change." Getting angry doesn't make a kid (or anyone else, for that matter) change their behaviour. So why do we so often think getting angry makes them change? Many parents warn and nag at their kid about doing or not doing a certain thing, and the kid ignores them. Then the parent—let's say it's dad—gets to the point where he's angry, so marches up to the kid and is about to take immediate action. But the kid is now in a big hurry to do what he or she was told. You can see why parents make the mistake of thinking that getting angry motivated the change. But it wasn't the anger; it was the fact that dad was about to act that brought the change from the kid.

Imagine a highway patrol officer standing on the side of the road without a radar gun or a traffic ticket book. Cars go speeding by and the police officer is very angry at the speeding, but his anger won't slow the drivers at all. The same police officer with a radar gun and a speeding ticket book will bring immediate effect, whether or not he's angry. In fact, when handing out discipline, the calmer you are and the less obviously angry you are, the more 'personal authority' you have. I know it's shooting for the ideal, but parents don't have to get angry to get their kids to do as they are told; they just need to take action.

It's worth thinking about what this looks like in a bit more detail. Firstly, if you discipline because you've lost your temper

---

21 Farrell and Gray, *The Boy Crisis*, p 136.
22 See focusonthefamily.com.

(and I know it happens sometimes; we're all human), then you have also lost your moral authority, or most of it. You won't be thinking clearly. If you've lost your temper, it's a very good idea to apologize to your kids when you've calmed down. I've done it, and kids are generally quick to forgive.

Secondly, don't discipline by shouting at kids. You're likely to intimidate or crush the spirit of some kids. They'll either be intimidated or, if they are a bit older and tougher, they will simply push back, either actively or (worse) passively. You'll harden them into resentment. That's the mistake the social justice warriors make: they shout at men. You win a man's heart, and a young man's heart (in fact, even a toddler's heart), by talking quietly with him; by speaking genuinely and respectfully, not by shouting.

Thirdly, don't discipline in front of other people or siblings. It's very important to let kids keep their dignity, so don't embarrass them in front of others. Kids can forgive and forget most mistakes in parenting, but it's very hard to forgive and forget when someone embarrasses or belittles you in front of others. That takes a long time to heal.

When a boy gets to a certain age, you need to be very careful about how you discipline him. Especially with teenagers, this must be done privately, quietly and calmly—essentially just the way you would speak to another man. If we want them to behave like young men, we need to treat them like young men. It's not easy to keep your cool, and I haven't always managed it myself, but it matters. Treat an adolescent boy like a young man and he is much more likely to rise to the challenge. (If you need to rebuke or correct another man, always do so privately.) Speak quietly, privately and with eye contact, and explain not just what the rules are but also the 'why' of the required behaviour. If possible, explain the relational reasons why the behaviour matters. For example, "You are not to belch around your mother because it is disrespectful to her". Think through how you would have 'the hard conversation' with another man, then talk this way with your son.

The apostle Paul says, "do not exasperate your children" (Eph 6:4). Literally, this means don't "provoke them to anger". Don't make them angry or frustrated by misusing your power. Let me mention a few ways that our power can be misused before offering a list of positive ways to engage with kids and family life.

- *Constant criticism:* If we constantly criticize our kids, pull them down, or make them feel like they can never perform well enough, we can crush their spirit.
- *Inconsistency:* Being inconsistent in discipline is a misuse of power. Laughing at something one day but punishing it the next day means a kid's whole world is uncertain. Kids need consistency; they need to know what the rules are and where they stand. It's also important to keep any promise you make to your children, as they need to learn they can trust you.
- *Loss of dignity and embarrassment:* As I said above, we can frustrate or anger our children by disciplining them in front of others. Feel free to praise in public, but discipline only in private. Whatever their age, you must always let them keep their dignity, as the pain of embarrassment lasts a lot longer than the actual discipline handed out.
- *Favouritism:* Perhaps the fastest way to exasperate a child is to show favouritism. If you favour one child over the others, you will hardwire anger and frustration into them.

There are so many ways to engage positively with kids, and they are so keen to engage back. It's really just a matter of applying our minds (and diaries) to the opportunities. Here are some possibilities to consider.

Regular family dinner nights
When the kids are smaller these can be most nights. As kids grow up, you can aim to schedule them weekly or more often if possi-

ble. Have a rule that no TV is on and no phones or devices are at the table so everyone is engaged in the present.[23] You can eat together and ask questions of the kids, like "What is something good that happened this week?" If you are a follower of Jesus, it's a great time to ask kids what they are thankful to God for, or to listen for anxieties. It's an opportunity to pray as a family, and for you as dad to read a part of the Bible (if the kids are little, it may be best to use a children's Bible). It may take some insistence to start this and to get the screens removed, but once you're in the routine it will be a highlight of family life.

One-on-one time

If your kids are still at school, you can arrange a special one-on-one time for each kid with dad. I used to take my kids—one at a time, one kid a week—to breakfast before school. It was a great time to just talk with them individually and listen to them about what was happening in their lives. If your work hours don't allow for a before-school breakfast, maybe you can do an afternoon tea, or lunch after sport on Saturday. This is golden time with your kids, so do it while they are younger and available. Once they've left home, they'll be a lot harder to catch. Their calendars will be as full as yours.

Family events

Think ahead about family events; plan a year or more ahead. How can you arrange events and routines that will build family traditions or legends? When our kids were young, we went on holidays to a beach house about a half-hour drive from my parents' home on the north coast of NSW. Same house, same beach for about ten years. The kids knew what we did at Christmas;

---

23 I would seriously suggest that you never have the TV or other screens on during any mealtime.

they looked forward to it, and still talk about it. Now in a different stage of life, as grandparents, we rent a beach house for any kids and grandkids who want to turn up—every year, same place. It's optional for them to come, but it's near the beach, it's free, and mum's food is good. They come and go as they please.

Are there traditions or regular fun things that your family can do together (sport, or camping, or board games, or movie nights, or surfing)? These times and memories will bond your family together.

Internet usage

Control what comes into your home via the internet. I don't have to tell you, but I will anyway—the internet will have a huge impact on your kids for good or ill. You need to help them control screen time in terms of both content and amount of time. The statistics on the internet's negative effect on young people, boys and girls, are staggering—whether it's social media, cyber bullying, video gaming, or pornography.

There are some simple rules that will help, such as putting the family computer in a central place where everyone will see it. Since almost everyone has their own device these days, you may choose to make 'no devices in bedrooms' a family rule. This may well cause a fight, but it will probably be worth it. Friends of mine have the family bedrooms upstairs in their home, so they have a rule that all phones and other devices go in a box downstairs before their owners go up to bed. Whatever rules you come up with, it's good to get on the front foot.[24]

---

24 Further reading: there are a huge range of resources on the website of the Australian eSafety Commissioner (esafety.gov.au). See also Zimbardo and Coulombe, *Man Disconnected*; M Carr-Gregg, *Beyond Cyberbullying: An essential guide for parenting in the digital age*, Penguin, 2013, pp 137-148; Sax, *Boys Adrift*; and L Sax, *Girls on the Edge: Why so many girls are anxious, wired, and obsessed— and what parents can do*, 2nd edn, Basic Books, 2020.

Reading

One of the great joys of having younger kids is the opportunity to read to them. The ideal time is before they go to bed. If you're not a great reader, practise—you'll improve quickly, and your kids will love it. Steve Biddulph says:

> By reading, kids learn that life can make sense. They learn the language by which they can think. They discover lives have stories, [and] we can choose a good or bad story for ourselves. They can see that all behaviours have underlying reasons, and there is an internal, non-tangible world of feelings that can be navigated safely. You don't learn a lot about feelings by watching TV because you usually only see the actions, not the reasons. And on TV the language is simplified.[25]

Depending on the age of your kids, there's a huge range of great books to read them. Some of my kids' favourites are:

- *The Magic Faraway Tree* and *The Wishing Chair* series by Enid Blyton
- *Charlie and the Chocolate Factory, Matilda, Fantastic Mr Fox* and *James and the Giant Peach* by Roald Dahl
- The *Narnia* series by CS Lewis
- *The Hobbit* by JRR Tolkien

Rough-and-tumble play

If you watch dads play with their kids, they play differently from mums. In particular, they are more likely to play rough-and-tumble games. American authors refer to this as 'roughhousing': wrestling, physically testing one another. All kids, but especially and very importantly boys, love to wrestle. Bettina Arndt has

---

25 Biddulph, *Raising Boys in the Twenty-First Century*, p 65.

posted an interesting discussion between Jordan Peterson and Warren Farrell on the importance of rough-and-tumble play for children, especially boys.[26] Often mums have no idea why this has to happen, but it's very significant especially for little boys. In fact, it seems hardwired into male DNA, and not just human males; young male chimpanzees "are significantly more likely to engage in aggressive rough-and-tumble play than are young females".[27] These games are where kids, especially boys, learn how to use their strength and aggression, but in the right way; to keep within the boundaries, to have fun without actually hurting other people, to control anger, to lose the game but keep control of their emotions. Dad is part of the fun, but is also modelling self-control:

> The aim is to coach them in how to be energetic, excited and lively but always safe. A potent lesson is being learnt here. When the boy is grown up, he will almost inevitably be stronger and larger than his girlfriend or wife. He must know how to take criticism, experience strong emotions and, at the same time, never use his physical strength to dominate or hurt her. The boy learns to contain his strength from his father who never hurts him and doesn't allow him to hurt others.[28]

The "training and instruction of the Lord"

Returning to Ephesians 6, we find the *third* and final—and most important—of our observations: Paul tells fathers to *bring up*

26 B Arndt, 'Jordan Peterson on roughhousing' [video], *Bettina Arndt*, YouTube, 24 May 2018, accessed 7 January 2022 (youtube.com/watch?v=ryVSSOq2FCM).
27 Sax, *Boys Adrift*, p 29.
28 Biddulph, *The New Manhood*, pp 163-164. See also Farrell and Gray, *The Boy Crisis*, pp 142, 144-145; Sax, *Boys Adrift*, p 29; and Sax, *Why Gender Matters*, pp 53-55.

their children in the training and instruction of the Lord. In the original language, this literally means to nourish and feed them. And the way you feed a child's soul is through encouragement.

Words of encouragement help children to grow and give them confidence. If you are a follower of Jesus, I know it will be your heart's desire to bring your children up "in the training and instruction of the Lord". If you're a Christian dad, it's your job to teach them about Jesus. You're not doing this alone, but you can't subcontract it all out. Ideally, your wife will be your key partner in this and there will also be Sunday school (or kids' church, or whatever it's called in your neck of the woods) with teachers and youth leaders who will help you. But, dad, it's your job. You have to see that it's happening as much as you can, and you have to be aware of how the process is going.

This is more than just teaching them the rules about living, or the Old Testament stories, although these are important. The Bible is talking about modelling a living trust in Jesus to your kids, as much as it is possible for you. Show them that you're living your life with a real faith or trust in Jesus and that this affects every aspect of life. Build this into ordinary life; as Moses urged the people of Israel, "Talk about [God and his commandments] when you sit at home and when you walk along the road, when you lie down and when you get up" (Deut 6:7). If Moses was writing that today, he'd say, "Talk about it as you take them to school and when you pick them up from music lessons and when you teach them to drive". Build teaching about the Lord into your family's routine, like mealtimes and bedtimes. For example, as I said above you can simply have a routine of reading a small part of the Bible after dinner and asking the kids for one thing they (or you) can pray about.

You can teach your children and set an example, but, in the end, they have to make their own decisions as they grow. You might be filled with heartache about being a dad, and fathering might not work out the way you'd want. All you can do is be the best dad you can be, set the best example that you can, and pray for your children. Ultimately, they have to live out their own life, because it's their story. You may have children who grow up and, as young adults, reject the faith of their parents, either actively or passively. This is a real heartache that many Christian parents carry with them. If this is you, I have no clichéd answers; I simply say that you have to play the long game, be patient, and live a consistent Christian life. Keep the relationship door as open as possible, be gentle in how you speak with them, and pray that God will be at work in their lives (which will often happen through people other than you).

Obviously, there is much more that can be said about being a dad, and there are specifics about raising boys and raising girls.[29] And of course, parenting changes when your kids have grown. You'll always be their dad, but much of this chapter has been about parenting younger kids on the journey to adulthood. If this journey goes well and your kids are responsible and functional adults, your influence with them changes over time; you'll move from issuing instructions to offering advice or suggestions as appropriate. Best of all, they may ask your opinions on life matters. You move from captain of the ship to a consultant and encourager.

The message of this chapter is that being a dad is vital in the life of your kids. What they need most is for you to man up, turn up, and get involved. Love them. Be around as much as you can, know where those big marker buoys are, and you'll be able to work it out day by day. They need you.

---

29 Steve Biddulph's books on raising boys and girls are both excellent: *Raising Boys in the Twenty-First Century* and *Raising Girls in the Twenty-First Century.*

Lessons from a divorced dad

By Andrew

I became close to K after one of my best friends committed suicide during end-of-school exams. This incident had a profound impact on me and our close group of friends. K and I ended up in a relationship when I was 19; she was already a mother to two kids, a two-year-old and a three-month-old.

Studying part-time to obtain an accounting and law degree, raising two kids (with another on the way), struggling at part-time jobs to pay the bills, all while trying to maintain my relationship, was incredibly hard work. There were many happy times, but the pressure and stress were often overwhelming. Rightly or wrongly, I felt like the success or otherwise of the family rested solely on me.

I finally graduated with an accounting degree and a law degree when I was 26 and commenced a job with a large national financial advisory and insolvency firm. The next four years involved working, studying, raising (now) four kids, and having almost my entire wage consumed in rent by the monster that is Sydney housing.

At age 30, K and I had our third child, making it five kids in total that we were raising. Around this time, K's sister had a premature baby at about 21 weeks and K's father was sentenced to jail for a white-collar crime. It was at this point that all the pressures of life had built up and our relationship imploded. It didn't explode in a supernova as such; it was more of a collapse into a black hole, and we separated. Our youngest daughter was just a few months old. More than a decade's worth of immense pressure overwhelmed us.

The next couple of years were a very difficult period. I was trying to navigate the break-up, raise young kids, work, and undertake further study. To a large extent I had also lost my relationship with K's family and my step-kids, who had filled my life for more than ten years. There were a number of times I thought I would only have minimal custody of my kids. Luckily, however, I have been able to have the kids from Thursday to Sunday, so I have been able to develop strong bonds with them. During this time, although I felt like I was being thrown around in black rampaging seas, my sole focus was on the kids, spending time with them and stabilizing things as much as possible. When I wasn't with them, I sometimes had great difficulty dragging myself out of bed and getting to work, but I would think, "If I don't do this for the kids, who will?" So onto the long and lonely train ride into Martin Place, up the escalators and into the office I would go.

I also became bitter about all the years I had spent studying accounting and law, feeling like it had got my family and me nowhere except saddled with a huge debt. I was in some mental and emotional turmoil, looking for answers, so I started reading and listening to philosophy, physics and maths.

At 32, I left the insolvency firm to work at an airline. It was there that I met a Christian.

I remember being amazed at how jolly he was. Talking to anyone about anything was like water off a duck's back to him. He introduced me to another Christian and we started reading the Bible together.

I started to realize that the only solution to the problem of life was Jesus, and all the philosophy, physics and maths theories I was reading led to dead ends. Jesus' teachings are the perfect reflection of what is happening in reality and human nature—he is the ultimate metaphysical philosopher! The more experience I have and observations I make in life, the more I think his teachings reflect the highest resolution of reality. The idea that Jesus is God is not some sort of fanciful leap of faith, but a logical conclusion; and all the poor, lost and lonely souls out there that may never have a loving relationship and kids (which I have always thought was one of life's biggest injustices) can have the ultimate loving relationship with God. I've also met a lot of great dads and Christians through City Bible Forum.

So, through all my experiences, what advice can I give to other dads who have experienced divorce? Here are my top 10 tips:

- Spend as much time with your kids as possible.
- Always tell the truth.
- The most important thing for kids is that they don't grow up with 'mess in their heads'. They can recover from disappointments, but it's harder to recover from manipulation, lies and sustained psychological pressure from parents.
- Don't project your own insecurities and fears onto your kids. Be aware of your own behaviour, and regulate.
- Never speak badly of ex-partners/families, but support them and the kids (including financially) as much as possible.
- Instil ethics, morals, a work ethic and a love of learning in kids, as well as a love of fun, joy, laughter, creativity and music.

- Even if things are desperate, be strong for your kids; laugh with your kids.
- A fool's hope is still hope; if you still have fingernails, you can hang on.
- Accept the difficulties and vicissitudes of life, lose honourably, and carry on anyway.
- Be open with your kids, and if you make a mistake don't be too proud to apologize.

More recommended resources on being a dad

Boys and ADHD

- *The Boy Crisis: Why our boys are struggling and what we can do about it* by Warren Farrell and John Gray (BenBella Books, 2018), pages 314-386.
- *Raising Boys in the Twenty-First Century: How to help our boys become open-hearted, kind and strong men* by Steve Biddulph (revised edition, HarperCollins, 2018), pages 198, 202 and 228.
- *Boys Adrift: The five factors driving the growing epidemic of unmotivated boys and underachieving young men* by Leonard Sax (Basic Books, 2007), pages 41, 110, 114-118, 238 and 241-249.

Screen time and video games

- *Boys Adrift* by Leonard Sax, pages 77, 80-82, 85, 92, 94, 172-178 and 306.
- *Man Disconnected: How technology has sabotaged what it means to be male* by Philip Zimbardo and Nikita D Coulombe (Rider Books, 2015), page 128.
- *Raising Boys in the Twenty-First Century* by Steve Biddulph, pages 142-143.

Social Media

- *Why Gender Matters: What parents and teachers need to know about the emerging science of sex differences* by Leonard Sax (second edition, Harmony Books, 2017), pages 163-169.
- *The New Manhood: Love, freedom, spirit and the new masculinity* by Steve Biddulph (revised edition, Simon & Schuster, 2019), page 163.

Bullying

- *Why Gender Matters* by Leonard Sax, pages 63 and 66-68.
- *Raising Boys in the Twenty-First Century* by Steve Biddulph, pages 160-161.
- *Beyond Cyberbullying: An essential guide for parenting in the digital age* by Michael Carr-Gregg (Penguin, 2013).

Housework

- *Raising Boys in the Twenty-First Century* by Steve Biddulph, pages 115-120.

Pornography

- *Raising Boys in the Twenty-First Century* by Steve Biddulph, page 139.

Sport

- *Raising Boys in the Twenty-First Century* by Steve Biddulph, pages 185-188.
- *The Boy Crisis* by Warren Farrell and John Gray, page 94.

CONCLUSION: FOLLOWING THE GREATEST MAN

WHEN I TALK ABOUT Jesus with men who aren't his follow-ers, I know very often they're thinking, "It's alright for women and kids, but not for me—not for a man". It grieves me that so often the Christian faith has been presented in a way that reinforces this. Jesus has been 'feminized'. We have dressed up ministers in frocks and funny hats, and some church services have become ethereal pantomimes. Jesus is presented in stained-glass windows, looking sickly and snuggling a lamb. Churches sing songs that make it sound like 'Jesus is my boyfriend', and there's talk about falling in love with this wonderful man. May God forgive us.

If you're not a follower of Jesus, I simply ask you to read one of the four Gospels and look for the man, Jesus.[1] If ever there was a role model of healthy masculinity, he's the one. I don't mean he's a 'real man' because he worked half his life as a tradie.[2] I mean his character: strong on the truth, gentle with the weak, fearless in standing up for the little people, selfless, courageous, calm under pressure. He cares for his family and has time and compassion for the little people. Can you imagine the courage it took for him to deliberately walk the full length of his country

---

1   There are four accounts of Jesus' life at the start of the New Testament: the accounts written by Matthew, Mark, Luke and John. Christians refer to these biographical accounts of Jesus' life as 'Gospels'.
2   Australian for 'tradesman'.

knowing that, at the end of the hundred-plus-kilometre walk, he would be crucified?

Jesus is history's greatest example of a man stepping up to take care of people. He calls men to follow him as Lord and master, but also as friend and brother. He calls 'his men' to commit their lives day by day to caring for others and taking the message of forgiveness to a dying world, to make a difference that will last into eternity. It's a message that should naturally resonate with men.

But it's worth looking in a bit more depth at the truth of this message, and the hope and purpose it offers us as men.

The message of Jesus is *true*

"What is truth?" asked Pontius Pilate, the Roman administrator of Judea from AD 26-36 (John 18:38). Famous words, which were no doubt spoken in cynical, eye-rolling frustration. Jesus being on trial was a political problem for Pilate, and he just wanted the problem to go away. But notice what Jesus said as he looked Pilate in the eye:

> "You are a king, then!" said Pilate.
>
> Jesus answered, "You say that I am a king. In fact, the reason I was born and came into the world is to testify to the truth. Everyone on the side of truth listens to me."
>
> "What is truth?" retorted Pilate. (John 18:37-38)

Jesus said, "Everyone on the side of truth listens to me". Rather than begin a great philosophical discussion, let's use a working definition of 'truth' from *Webster's Dictionary*: "Conformity to fact or reality; exact accordance with that which is, or has been, or shall be". That definition will do for now.

In most areas of life, we simply believe that whatever lines up with reality is true. But this often doesn't apply to the way people think about 'the spiritual realm' or spirituality. In anything spiritual, truth can seem totally subjective. It's seen as being about 'what works for me' or 'what I feel like believing'. Why not just believe what feels good for you and reject what you don't like? After all, there's a smorgasbord of different beliefs out there. Sadly, many people in Australia treat religion or spiritual matters as a joke; in the 2016 census, almost 48,000 Australians listed their religion as 'Jedi'.[3]

Many people today choose to reject the Christian faith because they don't like what they think it offers. Their decision is entirely based on preference, not on truth or facts, because the assumption is that if it's spiritual or religious it can't be objectively verifiable—that is, you can't really know if it's true or false.

That is actually the case for the vast majority of spiritual beliefs or teachings. Why? Because almost all religious or spiritual claims rely on private visions or revelations that the leader or founder alone claims to have experienced. The teacher or founder receives a vision or a dream or an inspiration, then they tell others about it or write it down. Take Islam as an example: Muhammad claims that he was given a revelation from God, receiving it directly from the angel Gabriel (but privately, in a cave)—and that's how the Qur'an came to be written. In the same way, Joseph Smith claimed he wrote the Book of Mormon when the angel Moroni gave him golden tablets, which he was able to translate with special glasses. Then the golden tablets and the glasses disappeared.

So how can you prove these spiritual claims to be true or otherwise? You can't. They were private events that can't be verified or disproved either way. So we're back to either "I like it" or "I don't like it". *The* truth (as opposed to *your* truth or *my* truth) doesn't really come into the equation.

---

3   Australian Bureau of Statistics, *Census reveals Australia's religious diversity on World Religion Day* [media release], ABS, 18 January 2018, accessed 7 January 2022 (abs.gov.au/AUSSTATS/abs@.nsf/mediareleasesbyReleaseDate/8497F7A8E7DB5BEFCA25821800203DA4).

But the Christian gospel is in a different category; it's based on something altogether different.[4] The Christian message claims to be objectively, historically true. It is based on events that really happened, in public, with eyewitness accounts written down. We usually call it 'history'.

Historical truth

There are different ways of establishing the truth. For example, there's mathematical truth (logic within a system), or scientific truth (repeatable experiments). In history, we look at the accounts of different eyewitnesses, or of those who recorded the words of eyewitnesses in various documents, to weigh up the evidence and work out what really happened. It's a similar process to what happens in a criminal law court: witnesses are called, evidence is weighed, and decisions are made.

Christianity isn't based only on private revelations to spiritual leaders, but on public, historical events that happened in real time and space, as witnessed by many people, some of whom wrote down what happened. That's what the first four books of the New Testament are: eyewitness testimonies to the birth, life, teachings, death and resurrection of Jesus, at a particular time and place.

Take the Gospel of Luke, for example. Luke was a doctor, and unusually among the New Testament writers he wasn't Jewish. He travelled a lot with the apostle Paul on his missionary journeys. He tells us at the beginning of his account of Jesus' life that what he writes is based on eyewitness accounts:

Many have undertaken to draw up an account of the things that have been fulfilled among us, just as they were handed

---

4   You might notice that in some places I've used the word 'Gospel', with a capital 'G', while in other places I've referred to the 'gospel' with a small 'g'. The convention within a lot of Christian writing is for 'Gospel' to refer to each of the four New Testament biographies of Jesus, while 'gospel' refers to the 'good news'—the overall message about Jesus. I'm following that convention here.

down to us by those who from the first were eyewitnesses and servants of the word. With this in mind, since I myself have carefully investigated everything from the beginning, I too decided to write an orderly account for you, most excellent Theophilus, so that you may know the certainty of the things you have been taught. (Luke 1:1-4)[5]

Luke begins with the story of Jesus' birth in the first two chapters of his Gospel. When he gets to the beginning of Jesus' public life, which began when Jesus was about the age of 30, Luke goes all out, giving us information on the historical setting and the political leadership of the time:

In the fifteenth year of the reign of Tiberius Caesar—when Pontius Pilate was governor of Judea, Herod tetrarch of Galilee, his brother Philip tetrarch of Iturea and Traconitis, and Lysanias tetrarch of Abilene—during the high-priesthood of Annas and Caiaphas, the word of God came to John son of Zechariah in the wilderness. (Luke 3:1-2)

Luke couldn't say 'AD 30'—obviously that date system wasn't in operation yet. But AD 30 is what he was describing in his statement. He located his account at an exact point in time so readers could investigate and confirm his claims for themselves. He went out of his way to make clear that this was a real historical event. Even now, we can pinpoint the rulers and events he describes in history. In fact, Jesus had direct interaction with a number of these men during his public life.

Luke's account also lines up with the histories of the time from outside the Bible. For example, Josephus was a first-century Jewish historian who wasn't a Christian, so he had no reason to

---

5   We're not sure who Theophilus was. He may have been Luke's patron who supported him while he did the research and writing for this Gospel.

lie about the events he recorded.[6] There's a whole lot of detail in Josephus' accounts about events in the Jewish world that dovetail with the New Testament accounts. In fact, each of the rulers and politicians mentioned in Luke's statement above is mentioned in Josephus' history.

The point is this: the events described in the New Testament concern real events in real time and space. The New Testament invites you to investigate and see that the events really happened—they are 'true' records in the sense that they line up with reality. If the events didn't happen (and I'm especially talking here about the resurrection of Jesus), then Christianity falls over. It claims to be objectively, verifiably, historically true—*the* truth, not just *my* truth—so either it is or it isn't. It's not hard to check out the historical evidence and how the New Testament dovetails with other histories of the time.[7]

So the history is solid. And yet the message is much more than just events in history past. These events affect our lives, both now and in the future. This is God himself stepping into our broken world so we can know him, so we can be forgiven, and so we can have real hope for the future.

Jesus gives the *hope* we desperately need

On August 5th, 2010, a mining disaster in the San Jose goldmine in northern Chile made news around the world. Thirty-three miners were trapped 600 metres underground, as if the whole mountain they were working under had shuddered and moved.

---

6   The complete works of Josephus can be found and searched at ccel.org/ccel/josephus/complete/complete.

7   For more on the historical evidence for the life, death and resurrection of Jesus, see P Barnett, *Is the New Testament History?*, Authentic Media, 2002; and J Dickson, *The Christ Files: How historians know what they know about Jesus*, Zondervan, 2010.

They were stuck underground for a total of 69 days. The whole world rallied around to help, and eventually rescuers came up with the idea of bringing the miners up one at a time in a capsule that looked like a torpedo. It took 15 minutes to drag each of the miners up individually in the capsule, and all 33 were saved. Their wives or girlfriends were waiting for them, and everyone was really happy to get to the surface (except perhaps for one guy, who found both his wife and his girlfriend waiting for him). They even made a movie about the rescue called *The 33*, starring Antonio Banderas.

It's a great story with a happy ending, but here's what's really interesting: when the mountain first moved, the trapped miners made a kind of emergency room deep underground. They had a few days' food, but no idea if they would ever be found. After 16 days, some of them were considering suicide and some were considering cannibalism (I guess those two alternatives could work together, but it's hard to imagine how desperate they were). But on the 17th day, something happened: a little shaft drilled from the surface finally broke through, putting light into the 'emergency room'. The miners knew they would eventually be rescued. That ray of light from the surface kept them going for another 52 days. Imagine: 52 days—69 days in total!

What was it that kept them going? After 17 days, they finally had *hope*.

Once you know what the future holds, it affects your present in a huge way. 'The 33' hold the record for the longest time underground after a mine disaster before being safely rescued. They held on for so long because they had hope. As we live in this broken world, we all long for hope; what we believe about the future has a vital effect on how we live today.

One man who really understood hope was Viktor Frankl, a Jewish psychiatrist who was born in Austria in 1905 and spent the last three years of World War II locked up in Nazi concentration camps. Much of that time was spent in death camps like Auschwitz. I had thought that people's survival in the death camps was really just random. But as Frankl explains in his book *Man's Search for Meaning*, something much more significant was at work. Frankl committed himself to keeping fellow prisoners alive. But how?

> [By] giving [the fellow prisoner] inner strength by pointing out to him a future goal to which he could look forward. Instinctively some of the prisoners attempted to find one on their own. It is a peculiarity of man that he can only live by looking to the future—*sub specie aeternitatis*. And this is his salvation in the most difficult moments of his existence. ...
>
> The prisoner who had lost faith in the future—his future—was doomed. With his loss of belief in the future, he also lost his spiritual hold; he let himself decline and became subject to mental and physical decay. Usually this happened quite suddenly, in the form of a crisis, the symptoms of which were familiar to the experienced camp inmate. We all feared this moment—not for ourselves, which would have been pointless, but for our friends. Usually it began with the prisoner refusing one morning to get dressed and wash or to go out on the parade grounds. No entreaties, no blows, no threats had any effect. He just lay there, hardly moving. If this crisis was brought about by an illness, he refused to be taken to the sickbay or to do anything to help himself. He simply gave up. There he remained, lying in his own excreta, and nothing bothered him anymore.[8]

Hope is essential for life—certainly for a life that is more than just existing.

8   V Frankl, *Man's Search for Meaning* (I Lasch trans), Beacon Press, 2006 [1946], pp 72-74. This whole book is very important. It's not deliberately gruesome, but it is both troubling and worth pondering deeply.

You may want to think about your own life and what you hope for. There are many different ways of seeing the world, sometimes called a 'worldview'. A good question to ask as you consider different worldviews is: "What does this way of seeing the world say about hope for the future?"

Here's an example of testing a worldview from that angle: the Global Atheist Convention scheduled for February 2018 in Melbourne was entitled 'Reason for Hope'. Author Salman Rushdie was to be the keynote speaker. If you don't remember reading about the events at the convention, that's because it was cancelled. The website announced, "Ticket sales have been substantially below expectations and below levels of previous conventions so unfortunately, the convention cannot proceed."[9] I'm not gloating, and I don't think all those atheists rushed off to churches to become Christians. But I can't help but wonder—have people begun to think through the fact that, if you chase the rabbit down the rabbit hole of reasoning from the atheistic worldview, there is absolutely no "reason for hope"? None. Richard Dawkins has famously said, "The universe we observe has precisely the properties we should expect if there is, at bottom, no design, no purpose, no evil and no good, nothing but blind, pitiless indifference."[10] So, have a nice day!

It's interesting that it's basically impossible to be thoroughly consistent in living out this worldview. We just can't live in tune with the idea that the world is about "blind, pitiless indifference". We keep looking for meaning and hope. We know instinctively that people matter, and right and wrong matters.

The Bible's worldview, the message of Jesus, offers real hope

9   M Gryboski, 'Atheist convention featuring Richard Dawkins canceled over poor ticket sales', *The Christian Post*, 8 November 2017, accessed 7 January 2022 (christianpost.com/news/atheist-convention-featuring-richard-dawkins-canceled-over-poor-ticket-sales.html).

10 R Dawkins, *River Out of Eden: A Darwinian view of life*, Basic Books, 1995, p 133.

to those who will embrace it—to those who will embrace *him* by trust.

Summarizing the Bible's message in a couple of pages is a bit like reducing the Grand Canyon to a 6x4 postcard, but here goes:

There is a personal Creator, the God of the Bible, who has created humanity to know him and live by trusting him. Human beings are inherently valuable, made in the image of God, but humanity has walked away from God our Creator. We ignore the one who gives us life and spend our lives trying to fill up the hole in our souls with other things. This is not just empty but offensive to God; it's the opposite of trusting him. God warns us that, at the end of a lifetime of ignoring him and shutting him out of our lives, the consequences will fit the crime. God will give us the deserved endpoint of what we've done: he will shut us away from himself for eternity. Jesus' word for that is "hell": empty, lonely, hopeless and Godless.

The God of the Bible is a God of justice. The penalty for disobeying, ignoring and dishonouring the God who gives life is that we will die, not just physically but spiritually and eternally.

I realize this is an unpopular teaching these days (it probably always has been). But Jesus took it very, very seriously. He warned again and again about an eternal separation from God. He pleaded with people to listen to him, and to avoid facing God's judgement unforgiven. And he makes the same plea to us today in the pages of the Bible.

This book is unbalanced. If you've waded through all the chapters, you've read tens of thousands of words about masculinity and how to live as a man. Well done. And now this very short section, about God's eternal judgement on those who ignore him, is just a couple of hundred words long. But this issue dwarfs every other decision any of us will ever make. It is a matter of eternal life and death. I cannot urge you strongly enough to take Jesus' warnings seriously. As the apostle Paul says, "We implore you on Christ's behalf: Be reconciled to God" (2 Cor 5:20).

The God of the Bible is a judge. But (and aren't you glad there's a "but"?) he is also merciful. And he longs to forgive people and bring them back to himself.

How can God be 'just' (his laws matter, actions have consequences) and 'merciful' (forgiving, wiping the slate clean, removing guilt) at the same time? The only answer is that God himself pays the penalty that his law demands and that people deserve.

That is the message of the New Testament. God stepped into our world in the person of Jesus. He came to show us God's character and to teach us about God, but most importantly he came to die in our place so that we can be forgiven and brought into friendship with God.

God can be just *and* merciful. The price has been paid. The apostle Peter recounts it like this: "'He himself bore our sins' in his body on the cross, so that we might die to sins and live for righteousness; 'by his wounds you have been healed'" (1 Pet 2:24). Jesus paid the price of forgiveness by suffering the death humanity deserved. The penalty is paid, and so Jesus was raised to life again. Jesus' promise now is that those who will trust him will be forgiven, and that God will give his Spirit to those people who put their trust in Jesus. The Spirit of God (the Holy Spirit) will begin to transform those who belong to Jesus so that we can "live for righteousness", as Peter puts it. He will begin to change us to be like Jesus.

Those who trust and follow Jesus will change, yet we will always be a work in progress. But being a 'work in progress' doesn't jeopardize our salvation; that's secured once and for all when we trust in Jesus and his death for us. The process of becoming more like Jesus isn't what wins forgiveness for us; it's what flows from the forgiveness that we already have in Jesus.

Jesus promised that he would return one day and bring the 'judgement day'. Everyone will be judged according to how they have responded to the knowledge of God they had. For those who have trusted Jesus as their Lord, there is the promise of eternal life in a new creation, where there will be no more mourning or crying or pain.

This is the *hope* that Jesus offers—a sure and certain hope for the future that transforms every part of life in the here-and-now.

To know God and find forgiveness means we must acknowledge our sin and ask for forgiveness because Jesus died in our place to take our guilt. We must acknowledge Jesus as our Lord and master, and live our lives trusting him.

I became a follower of Jesus over 40 years ago by praying a prayer just like the one below. These aren't magic words, but God promises that he will certainly hear a person whose heart reaches out to him in this way.

Dear God,

I know that I am not worthy to be accepted by you. I don't deserve your gift of eternal life. I am guilty of rebelling against you and ignoring you. I'm sorry, and I need your forgiveness.

Thank you for sending your Son, Jesus, to die for me so that I may be forgiven. Thank you that he rose from the dead to give me new life.

Please forgive me and change me, so that I may live with Jesus as my ruler. Amen.

Jesus gives us *purpose* and calls us to live for something bigger than just ourselves

Every human being lives for something. We all have something at the centre of our lives. We have desires, things we love, and things we long for. Our longings drive us or pull us along. Two of the most common and fundamental longings for human beings are *security*—the desire to be safe or protected—and *significance*—the desire to feel that we matter, that we are noticed, appreciated and respected.

For most men, it's the desire to feel significant that matters. Alain de Botton insightfully says that the desire for status is another way of wanting the love of the world around us:

> Every adult life could be said to be defined by two great love stories. The first—the story of our quest for sexual love—is well known and well charted, its vagaries form the staple of music and literature, it is socially accepted and celebrated. The second—the story of our quest for love from the world—is a more secret and shameful tale. If mentioned, it tends to be in caustic, mocking terms, as something of interest chiefly to envious or deficient souls, or else the drive for status is interpreted in an economic sense alone. And yet this second love story is no less intense than the first, it is no less complicated, important or universal, and its setbacks are no less painful. There is heartbreak here too, suggested by the distant, resigned eyes of many whom the world has elected to dismiss as nobodies.[11]

It's this desire for the love of the world around us that drives men to want to achieve, to be noticed, to win at work or at sport, to have the money, the house, the car, and the girlfriend. The desire to feel significant isn't wrong; the problem comes when we try to meet that desire with stuff that won't last or will never quite deliver, or in ways that damage ourselves and other people.

Jesus calls men to follow him, and he gives those men significance. His men are valued so much that Jesus has died for them, and their significance comes from being "sons of God" (Gal 4:6; Heb 2:10). Jesus calls these men his "friends" (John 15:13) and

11   de Botton, *Status Anxiety*, pp 13-14.

even his "brothers" (Matt 28:10; Rom 8:29). But as he gives his men such significance in the eyes of God, he calls them to live their lives for something much bigger than selfish ambition or an easy life. He gives men work to do that will have value into eternity: to "seek first his kingdom and his righteousness" (Matt 6:33). Jesus promises great rewards (eternal rewards, in fact) for those who will live a life trusting him (e.g. Matt 25:14-30; Luke 14:13-14).

So, what will it look like to live as a man seeking Jesus' kingdom and righteousness? It will mean working to see Jesus' rule in our own lives and the lives of others. One part of that will be a commitment to Jesus' people gathering as a community. The word 'church' in the New Testament is simply the word for a 'gathering'.[12] A church is the 'gathering' of the people who follow Jesus. They gather to hear Jesus' words taught or explained, and to encourage and care for (love) one another. It needs to be a community that takes Jesus' words, the Bible, seriously (especially the leaders of the church), and so focuses on engaging with the Bible when they meet.

Jesus doesn't call his men to be Robinson Crusoe; he calls them to be part of a community. So, if you're a man who follows Jesus, you need a church—a regular gathering that meets as Jesus' people. When you meet with them in larger groups or smaller groups—or even when you meet with somebody one-to-one—your mission is simple: as a man who follows Jesus, encourage others to listen to Jesus and to care for people. It's vital to help other men who follow Jesus to keep going in trusting him and living for him. If you live a consistent life trusting the way Jesus said to live, other men (and women) will listen. I'm not saying you have to be perfect, just consistent. If you're not consistent, no-one will listen.

Men have power in many ways. We may have power in our

---

12 The Greek word is *ekklēsia*.

physical size and strength, or in relationships, or in finances; the list goes on. Healthy masculinity is about using whatever power we have to care for and nurture the people around us in all sorts of ways. To really care for people will cost; it will mean living sacrificially. The great irony is that when we man up, when we get this right, we realize that this is what we were made for. This is the great joy and privilege of being a man—to nurture and care for people. It shouldn't be a surprise that this brings such a sense of purpose and such deep satisfaction. After all, the greatest man who ever lived taught us that it's as we follow him and say 'no' to living selfishly that we will find life, both now and in eternity:

> "Whoever wants to be my disciple must deny themselves and take up their cross and follow me. For whoever wants to save their life will lose it, but whoever loses their life for me and for the gospel will save it." (Mark 8:34-35)

Jesus is alive today, and he calls us to trust him as our Lord and to man up.

Feedback on this resource

We really appreciate getting feedback about our resources—not just suggestions for how to improve them, but also positive feedback and ways they can be used. We especially love to hear that the resources may have helped someone in their Christian growth.

You can send feedback to us via the 'Feedback' menu in our online store, or write to us at info@matthiasmedia.com.au.

✿matthiasmedia

Matthias Media is an independent Christian publishing company based in Sydney, Australia. To find out more information about our resources, and to access samples and free downloads, visit our website:

www.matthiasmedia.com

How to buy our resources

1. Direct from us over the internet:
   – in the US: www.matthiasmedia.com
   – in Australia: www.matthiasmedia.com.au

2. Direct from us by phone: please visit our website for current phone contact information.

3. Through a range of outlets in various parts of the world. Visit **www.matthiasmedia.com/contact** for details about recommended retailers in your part of the world.

4. Trade enquiries can be addressed to:
   – in the US and Canada: sales@matthiasmedia.com
   – in Australia and the rest of the world: sales@matthiasmedia.com.au

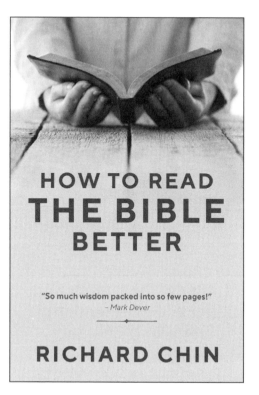